Dedication

I dedicate this book to my sister Julie who tragically passed away at 20 years of age. Julie is an inspiration to me. Due to her sudden loss at such a young age I decided to make the most of my life. I realised I had choices; sadly Julie's were taken away.

THE
Rich
Rules

Steps to
Wealth &
Happiness

THE
Rich
Rules
Steps to
Wealth &
Happiness

A Brief Introduction

The purpose of this book is to share my own experiences with you and my story of how I went from being homeless to becoming a multi-millionaire. I have purposefully written and edited every word even though I suffer from mild dyslexia. My grammar is far from perfect; however I feel you will engage with a far greater feeling for my journey through the written word from my own hand.

At 19 I was sleeping rough on the streets, and today I am one of the UK's largest property landlords and a multi-business owner. How did all this happen? What will you learn from reading this book? Well I'm going to share with you exactly how the whole process unfolded, so that you too can follow in my footsteps to achieve **Wealth and Happiness.**

Kindest Regards,
Kevin Green N.Sc

Make-A-Wish foundation exists for one reason – to grant magical wishes to children and young people fighting life-threatening conditions.

Our story started in 1986. Inspired by the story of Chris Greicius, a young boy fighting leukemia in the US, Make-A-Wish UK was formed to grant magical wishes to seriously-ill children in the UK.

We worked from offices above a shop in the town of Camberley, Surrey, and relied on the generous support of local volunteers to help us grant wishes. We granted four wishes in our first year. The very first wish was granted to Anthony from Liverpool, who went on a magical trip with his family to meet the Disney characters in Disney World Florida. As word spread about our work, more and more people began coming forward to volunteer their time. In our second year, we granted 13 wishes. We took on our first full-time member of staff in 1989. By the end of our fourth year, with the support of a growing team of passionate volunteers, we granted 100 magical wishes. Our volunteers would spend nearly every weekend out and about across the country – giving presentations, accepting cheques, and spreading the word about Make-A-Wish. As more families turned to us, we began setting up regional offices and taking on even more volunteers so we could keep granting wishes. There was never a dull moment.

We are still based in Camberley today, employing 50 members of staff. And volunteers are still at the heart of our organisation – their kind support has helped us grant over 9,000 magical wishes to date. But we need your help to keep granting more. Find out how you can become a volunteer or other ways you can support us and read about some of the magical wishes we've granted.

See website: http://www.make-a-wish.org.uk

Best wishes

Kevin Green.

According to my team, my job title is 'The Head of Happiness' .This name was given to me by my team as I have a habit of asking them if they are happy.

Take a look at my **WEALTH and HAPPINESS MONITOR** below and read on to find out how 'The Rich Rules' can help you.

To Steve my fellow entrepreneurial spirit and good friend, Thanks for everything!

WEALTH and HAPPINESS MONITOR

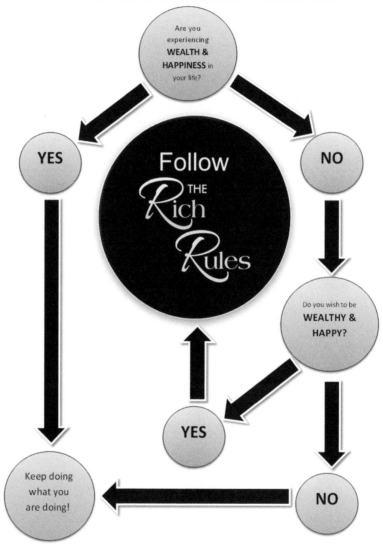

$\mathcal{R}$ich $\mathcal{R}$ule 1

Never waste a second of your time

It's an unorthodox way to begin, however, the **Wealth and Happiness** journey began with the death of my darling sister Julie.

She was 20 years old when she passed away after a very acute illness, which was a form of Leukemia called Lupus, in fact the correct term of the illness is Systemic Lupus Erythematosus (SLE). She went from being a very bright, happy and intelligent young girl to being 'taken away' very quickly, and of course that was a huge shock. I have no other brothers or sisters, so it was not only a particularly huge shock for me but also for my wonderful family. Due to that painful moment, I've always said to myself that I'd **never waste a second of my time**.

My sister Julie 1965-1985.

Ever since then, if I've ever felt unhappy about what may be happening, I've changed my outlook and my future, because for me happiness is a number one priority. Money has been a fortunate side benefit of building businesses around ideas which I am extremely passionate about. The journey has been quite a changeable one and has certainly not been easy. I am a self-made multi-millionaire, and that has come through damn hard work. Julie's sudden death and the resultant personal pain led to a change in my outlook on life; I said to myself, "I've got

choices in life, she had hers taken away," and pledged to myself the following:

"I'm going to use my time wisely and be the best that I can be at whatever I am doing."

This feeling is firmly embedded in me, I feel that all entrepreneurs have experienced pain somewhere in their life story and I'm certainly no exception in that department.

The other significant factor in my life that has been a massive help to me, is a lady I met called Sandie. She is a healer, and through my journey of becoming financially free, Sandie has had a huge influence on what's happened. I'll come back to how she has helped me in more detail a little later on.

I know this next revelation may sound a little weird to some, however, my sister has now become one of my 'spirit guides' and I feel like she is always with me in everything I do. Some of you will relate to that, and others will find it weird, and that's fine.

My childhood journey was an adventurous experience. I grew up with my sister, father and mother on a dairy farm. I wasn't very good academically in school, in fact I initially failed 'O' Level English, and 'O' Level Maths. I really didn't enjoy school at all, and as a result, I left school with very few academic qualifications. I remember my careers teacher asking me what I wanted to do after school. My reply was "I want to be a millionaire!" "How are you going to do that then?" he asked.

"Don't know." I replied.

He said, "Don't set your sights too high so you won't be disappointed!"

Those words stayed with me and I vowed one day I'd prove him wrong.

After completing secondary school my father suggested I attend a local agricultural college. I thoroughly enjoyed my time at Gelli Aur Agricultural College near Llandeilo, South Wales. I studied for a National Certificate in Agriculture, which taught me new ways to increase farm profits. I then suggested to my father that some of these might be a good idea to implement on the home farm, which was in South Wales. This didn't sit too well with him, and together with me being very headstrong it led to a bit of a clash between us. My father through his frustration gave me an ultimatum and I don't blame him! I either did it his way or it was going to be the highway!

Of course, I had to make a decision. Do I make my own way in life, or follow my father's wishes? I soon chose to make my own way following a hasty decision made in anger after my father returned home to the farm and ripped out an outside toilet I had spent time building to please him. He felt the toilet was facing the wrong way. This was what tipped me over the edge! My happiness with being at home had turned totally sour. I stupidly left home immediately and ended up on the streets, homeless. I made that decision without any clear forward planning whatsoever. I drove my Mark 2 Ford Escort, that I had built from scrap cars during my time on the farm, down the M4 motorway; I eventually ended up in the West Country in the town of Yeovil. I found an area of waste

land which was very sheltered and this is where I slept rough in my car.

This period lasted seven months before I landed myself a farm management job for Mr. Lawrence of Trill Farm Dairies in Longburton near Sherbourne. I didn't let on to my parents I was sleeping rough; they thought I already had a job, but there were occasions when I didn't have any money for food. I was begging lorry drivers for the chips off their plate in the transport café, and I'll never forget the kindness of some of those people who actually bought me a meal because they realised my predicament at that time. I have never forgotten their kindness; it's made me into the social entrepreneur that I am today. I love to help others whenever I can.

I really enjoyed working for Mr. Lawrence, and felt fortunate to have been chosen for that position of milking and managing the dairy herd on his farm. Unfortunately it was during that period that my sister died, she was 20 and I was 22. We actually shared our birthdays on the same date, namely, September 21st. I was extremely close to my sister, her passing made me realise that 'blood is thicker than water' and after her funeral I made amends with my father, in fact we hugged and cried. It was a wonderful reconciliation. I had always been close to my mother and the rest of the family, so it was good to get back on speaking terms and gain the respect of my father again. He suggested that I return to the home farm because I'd proved myself with Mr. Lawrence and done a great job managing the dairy herd there.

After a short while I returned home and increased the cow numbers on the home farm from 40 cows to 400 cows. During that period I met a wonderful lady, a farmer's daughter called Lynwen, and we got married. I carried on with what was really expected of me which was to continue picking up the mantel of dairy farming. I ran the farm well and reached all targets. My wife helped on the farm and we had three beautiful children, Llinos, Carwyn and Emyr. After achieving all my goals I began to feel frustrated, it wasn't REALLY what I wanted to be doing, I felt I was playing it safe. A real turning point in my life came after six years of married life on the farm. I remember I was in the milking shed one morning and there was a cow behind me who lifted her tail then coughed and pooped at the same time. This steamy cow dung came flying across the milking shed and filled up my ear and went all over my head. It stank and it was warm, but as it ran down my back and inside my shirt it turned cold. It was horrible! That was the moment when I said to myself, "I do not want to do this any longer."

The 400 cow herd at our home farm, Cwm Farm, Ferryside.

Saving money by dehorning cows ourselves, that's a young me on the right using a long cheese wire type dehorning method.

I had proven myself in farming, but my gut instinct, heart and soul were not in that particular career. It was a major decision for me to leave farming and go and find out what it was that I really wanted to do. During this period I was reflecting on my sister's death and realised I wasn't happy. Having made my pledge following Julie's passing, I needed to find **Happiness** and do something which I was going to love doing. Two major problems with that decision were that firstly my wife was not at all happy with that idea and secondly I also had to consider the effect a proposed change in career may have on our three beautiful children. If I left farming how was I going to provide financial security for them? I really didn't know what to do, but having learnt my lesson from my previous experience of leaving home without clear planning or decision making, I mulled this over for a long time.

It culminated with me applying for and being awarded a Nuffield Farming Scholarship. I won this award against all odds as there were other applicants who were highly academically qualified, unlike myself. The Nuffield Farming Scholarships Trust sponsored me to travel the world and study the attitudes and personalities of high achievers in business. This was a huge turning point for me, allowing me the opportunity to get out there in the wide world. However, my marriage was suffering hugely because of my intense desire to get away from farming as my wife was not at all happy with the idea of leaving farming. The scholarship was a vehicle to help me make the decision and shape the rest of my life and provide for our three beautiful children. As a result of my sister's death I didn't see any problem with me finding what I wanted in life but trying to do that without compromising other people around me was very difficult. I remember going for the interview at Nuffield. I was asked questions about my topic study and current affairs. It was a very intense interview from the leaders of the farming industry. I found myself sitting at the end of this huge long table and questions were being fired at me one after another from the various interviewers. I was aware that the interviewers were not supposed to respond to any of my answers and this was the case until I got about two thirds into the interview, and one interviewer asked a random question, "What do you think of the Teletubbies?" Of course my children were of an age where I knew all about the Teletubbies, and I immediately responded, "Tinky Winky is a little bit suspicious holding that handbag." The response was that virtually the whole of the interview panel fell into raucous laughter. I was told afterwards that it was that quick witted answer which won me the scholarship against all others who were better academically qualified than

myself. This is where I learned how important humour is in life.

The official remit of the scholarship was to return from the world tour with answers to help the farming industry. Also Nuffield encourage personal development in all of their scholars.

I visited New Zealand, Australia and Ireland and also carried out significant research in the UK. I was also looking outside the farming industry to find Chief Executives and Managers of major successful corporate business. I told the interview panel that I was going to interview Sir Richard Branson of Virgin and Bill Gates of Microsoft. They admired my high target, but I really didn't know whether I would achieve these goals. However, I felt in my heart that I would, and I would do whatever it took because I wanted to find out what made these leaders 'tick'.

One of my most important questions was 'Are entrepreneurs born, or can they be made?' The results of asking that question prompted interesting discussions, was it environment or genetics that determined success?

My study found that you don't need inherited genetics to become an entrepreneur. In fact, you just need to be in the right encouraging environment, with the will to achieve. This simple approach will lead to **Wealth and Happiness**.

The main lesson I learnt from the cow shed experience when I was pooped on by the cow, was:

'If the pain of where you are is not great enough, you will not change.'

As I embarked on my Nuffield Scholarship, I was not prepared to go back to farming. I was going to look out to the world industries and see what new career path I was going to take. I brought my wife along on part of the scholarship study, hoping that she would actually buy into my vision.

I wished to get into property and she didn't like this idea. She felt more comfortable with farming, and I could understand that, as it provided a certain amount of security, but I felt extremely frustrated in the farming industry and she was well aware of that.

Unfortunately, I was unable to change her mind, and that led to us separating amicably some two years later. We agreed our children should always be placed first in all decisions throughout the divorce proceedings. Fortunately my wife and I were able to talk sensibly at all times; she is a good woman and a fantastic mother.

When you want to make a difference in life, I feel you have to push forward and **follow your heart before your head**.

When you follow your heart you truly feel what you want to do, that's where your destiny is. If you follow your head you can get thrown off balance by only listening to your thinking voice, thoughts from the head often lead to ideas which are like a sticking plaster, i.e. like a sticking plaster which wears out and doesn't stay on for long, these ideas never last long term.

When you listen to your instinctive or feeling voice that comes from the heart you will find prosperity long term.

Some successful entrepreneurs are an example of people who do just that. They share my belief that when you want to make a difference in your life and begin living a life of prosperity and success, you must listen to your heart and not your head. I often hear how successful entrepreneurs follow their heart and gut instinct, and for me this was no exception as when I found property and trading, these businesses felt so right for me!

My mother and father luckily were very supportive of the whole idea of me actually leaving the farm for nine months and travelling the world, looking at best practice in the agricultural industry, and looking outside of agriculture into the corporate and business world. I subsequently left farming but this time it was with my father's consent and blessing. We formed a sensible business plan to exit dairying and rented the farm out.

When I went into property, my father always called my business the property 'thingy' and the outcome with the change in my father's thoughts is quite an interesting one. I'll describe later in **The Rich Rules** what happened with my father's business direction, and also to the outcome of my ex-wife.

$\mathcal{R}$ich $\mathcal{R}$ule 2

Self-awareness is the master key to success.

During my time at Nuffield Scholarship between 1999-2000, I found successful people are more aware and know themselves better than the 'average' person. I wanted to explore why two identical businesses being run by different individuals were achieving completely different success outcomes. I was fascinated by this, and wanted to get to know myself better as well. I also wanted to learn from people I admired. Many successful people like Mike Tilley of Merrill Lynch investment group told me that **travel is the University of Life.** The opportunity to travel and interview leading entrepreneurs was exciting and proved to be the vehicle for change in my life.

Other key questions I asked myself included 'What was it about the winners in business that were making their businesses thrive? Why were they better in some way? Was it their personality and attitude that made a difference to their **Wealth and Happiness?**'

This study really intrigued me, I looked at the mindset and energies of high achievers including their personalities and attitudes to determine whether entrepreneurs are born, i.e. is it their genetics, or can they be made, i.e. can the environment that one engages with shape the outcome of one's **Wealth and Happiness**.

The background to the study involved a lot of investigative work. During the research of psychology and whilst speaking to leading entrepreneurs in UK, I came across a gentleman called Roger Lovell. Roger was previously a personal adviser to Margaret Thatcher in Government on all strategic business based policies and he also wrote a book called Managing Change In The New Public Sector. Roger was a great influence on me during my research. There was so much information and he helped unravel the state of confusion I was in. He also helped me with the self-doubt that was beginning to creep in at the thought of travelling and interviewing high achievers. I was a little daunted to begin with.

I arranged to meet Roger at his house in Oxford and instantly warmed to his empowering personality. He reminded me of Hagrid from Harry Potter! He obviously was very 'high up' the political and life ladder and there was I, just a simple dairy farmer from South Wales. I knew on occasions in England for instance they thought I lived in such a remote part of Wales that we had only just discovered electricity!

Roger didn't view me as just a simple dairy farmer, he was very accommodating; at our first meeting Roger advised me that in order to achieve outcomes from a scholarship study and obtain tangible results I needed to be able to measure my findings. He suggested that I compiled some standard questions; the main ones I came up with are in the following list below. He explained that if I asked different questions of different people there wouldn't be a common denominator and therefore no clear and concise results. He suggested that if I wrote at least 25 common questions to ask each person I interviewed, then the results could be measured and published. I felt that this was marvelous advice, it simplified things for me.

Some of the key questions I used:-

- Are entrepreneurs born or can they be made?
- What is driving you?
- How good are your communication skills?
- How do you cope with change?
- How important do you think it is to have expertise of the industry?
- How willing are you to take risks?
- How persistent are you?
- Do you manage fitness to deal with stress?
- When you make a mistake, how do you deal with it and do you ever admit you are wrong?
- What really annoys you?
- How do you deal with negativity?
- Can you give me your favourite phrase?
- If you were granted a wish what would it be?
- What do you want to be remembered for at your funeral?
- What would you tell others who would wish to follow in your footsteps?

Nuffield kindly funded me to the tune of nine thousand pounds to cover the cost of my flights and accommodation. They also gave me what is referred to as 'The Nuffield Bible' which is a book of contacts of other Nuffield Scholars around the world. I found this extremely useful. I was mindful that other Nuffield scholars before me had used only the Bible and the list of contact names to interview other successful Nuffield's but hadn't ventured outside of the Nuffield framework. I was determined to interview Richard Branson and Bill Gates amongst others, just as I had told the Scholarship panel I would. Therefore, I wanted to go on a different path to everybody else, to get more into the corporate and business world because my desire was to find out what I wanted to do with the rest of my life. My wish was to experience exposure to as many different people in business as possible to help me decide on my future path in life.

I knew that it wasn't going to be the continuation of dairy farming after being pooped on by the cow in the milking shed! I also didn't feel comfortable being at the primary production end of the food chain, dairy farming was never fully in my heart and soul. I would keep a very open mind as I travelled the countries and then decide on my return as to what these businesses would be. It was more like a quest for the goblet of knowledge that I needed, and having pledged **'not to waste a second of my time'** for the rest of my life, I was excited about it.

For the organisational side of the Nuffield Scholarship study, it was the first time that I'd put a schedule together myself. I aimed for chief executives of major organisations. One of the key people who agreed to an interview was Mike Tilley of Merrill Lynch Investment Group, and I'd arranged to interview him in New Zealand as there were other leading entrepreneurs out there that I wished to try and get in contact with especially Sir Richard Branson, how was I going to track him down? Well I had a plan. I found out where he lived after a lot of investigation. I learnt he owned at least three residencies in the UK, with a main one near Oxford. I thought the first step was to follow the official route to engagement. I wrote to Virgin management and asked if it would be possible to interview Sir Richard Branson and outlined the reasons why I wished to interview him. I received a written reply from Virgin management which basically said 'yes we understand and acknowledge your request' and in so many words said if you're lucky that may happen one day, but there was no commitment of any form, so it was basically a 'warm' acknowledgement letter only. I needed to work a lot harder to make that interview happen, therefore, a couple of weeks later, the plan was to target Sir Richard Branson himself. He was my idol and I wanted to be like him. If there was any person that I looked up to and put on a pedestal, it was Sir Richard Branson.

I went to his house in my beat up old Citroen car, and parked around the corner so he wouldn't see it. I didn't have much money back then so I wore the best suit that I could afford. I went to the front gates, which were open, walked up to the house and knocked on the front door. A lady answered who I thought may be the housekeeper; little did I know how wrong I was. I asked her if I could meet Sir Richard Branson because I'd like to interview him for a scholarship study with Nuffield Farming Scholarship. She was very friendly in her response and she said that Richard was away abroad but was sure if I really wanted to interview Sir Richard that it would happen. I was rather perplexed by this statement from a 'housekeeper'. I went away and did some more research and when I googled Richard Branson and his background, I noticed a picture of this very same lady and it turned out to be Mrs Branson. I felt stupid because I hadn't known who she was when I met her face-to-face and I should have realised. I reflected on what a big mistake I'd made.

I then left it for about two weeks and I thought I'll go back on a Saturday, because he is likely to be in! I truly believed I was going to interview him and nothing was going to stop me, **I was going to do whatever it took** to get the interview.

I returned again on the Saturday two weeks later. I parked around the corner down by the canal and I walked up to the house. The gates were again wide open and I walked up to the front door, knocked on the door and the very same lady answered. I said I came two weeks ago. She replied yes she remembered me. I said my name is Kevin Green and I was really sorry but I hadn't realised that she was Mrs Branson, please could I interview her? She replied no, she didn't do interviews. I said fine I fully respect that; I really still wanted to interview Richard Branson, how would I make that happen? The reply was a little bit more positive this time. She said he's not here, in fact again he's not in the country, but if I came back in two Saturdays time he would be in the country and there was a chance that I may be able to interview him here.

Third time lucky I thought, this was going to be fantastic and I was really excited as the day got closer. Again I drove all the way down from Wales to Richard's house, this time I took my healer friend Sandie with me. I knocked on the door and again Mrs Branson opens the door. I'm very lucky to meet her three times in succession, I thought. She said that Richard was back here in the country but he'd had to go away on business for the day. The next thing that happened totally elated me, it was like I was in a pleasant dream.

"I've mentioned you to him and he's asked me to give you his mobile phone number and has asked if you don't mind could you ring his number at 6pm this evening?" she said.

She gave me his mobile number!

I thought this is fantastic and replied, "Thank you from the bottom of my heart and yes I will phone Richard at 6pm this evening, thank you so much for your help."

That day was a long day because Sandie and I had to wait for seven hours for that 6pm deadline to arrive. Exactly at 6pm I phoned the number and Sir Richard Branson answers the phone.

I could hardly get the words out of my mouth properly. I was speaking so fast I didn't make any sense.

Then I paused and said, "Sorry for fluffing, I'm just a bit excited. Sir Richard I'd love to interview you to find out what makes you tick as I'm doing a scholarship study on high achievers in business."

"Where are you?" he asked.

"We are down by the canal around the corner from your house," I replied.

He said, "Are you okay to come around to the house now and I'll do the interview with you straight away?"

Well I honestly said "Yes, yes, yes!" and you couldn't see my backside for dust. I went to the house in a whirlwind with Sandie following quickly behind, and there stood Sir Richard who took us into a large room.

We went into this big lounge where the table was the base of a redwood tree, the legs of the table were the roots and it was polished, it was huge! There were hand carved chairs that were placed around the table and a colourful tapestry hanging on the wall. All very minimal, no other clutter, there was hardly anything else in there, but it was still very welcoming.

Myself and Sir Richard in London 2012.

I got my questionnaire out and proceeded to go through the questions with Sir Richard, he was extremely accommodating. He ended up asking me more questions than I had actually asked him and he was challenging what I was doing. He was asking why I was determined to succeed. What was it that was driving me? I explained it was my sister's death and he understood that. I mentioned not wasting a second of precious time.

"Wow THAT sounds familiar!" he replied. Then he said, "You're going to be a lightworker."
At the time I didn't have a clue what that meant.

Richard answered all my questions and he then asked if there was any other way he could help me.

Well the whole evening took about two and half hours at his house to go through the interview. It was one of the best moments of my whole life and I felt so good actually coming away from the interview with all this information. One thing that struck me was I had put him on a huge pedestal; he actually seemed a very ordinary and down-to-earth person. It was quite profound really that I had built him up in my mind to be this magnificent person, which he is, but now he was no longer unreachable. He was somebody who had just gone out there and done it. He had got off his backside and against all odds he had achieved **Wealth and Happiness.**
Later on in **The Rich Rules** I will share some of the key strategies that Sir Richard

taught me. I've implemented these in my own businesses to create massive success.

A key belief I have learned from this experience is **you don't always have to reinvent the wheel**. If somebody is making something work, mirror that if it feels right to you.

The Bill Gates interview was very challenging, much more difficult to obtain. I was in the Consumer Electronics Show in Las Vegas and I knew through my research that Bill Gates usually appeared on the Microsoft stand every year.

How was I going to get an interview with him?

Well I'd asked around and I didn't have a clear plan, he was staying in the Bellagio Hotel and I did attempt to access the penthouse floor that he was staying on, but there was so much security all over the place I couldn't get anywhere near it. I'd received no response from Microsoft when I sent him my interview request letter, unlike Virgin.

With the confidence of having interviewed Sir
Richard Branson I thought ok, I've 'nailed'
that one and now I'm going to get this
interview with Bill Gates. The first day passed
by at the Consumer Electronics Show, it was
a mixed day. I was trying to find out what day
Bill Gates was likely to turn up at the show.
My intention was to just jump out in front of
him basically and ask "please can I interview
you" and explain what I wanted to achieve.
Then I had a stroke of luck. I posed as a press
reporter, wangled a press pass and bumped
into a gentleman who was working for the
press; he was working with a major
newspaper in America. He said that he'd
interviewed Bill Gates before and stated that
it's very difficult to get an interview with him
but he always appears on the Microsoft
stand.

On the second day of the show, he told me,
"If I were you I would wait there and you
may well get the interview."

I thought fantastic, thanked him very much,
raced around to the Microsoft stand and
befriended the Microsoft employees who

liked my Welsh accent. After approximately two hours of waiting, Bill Gates appeared by a side door right next to where I happened to be standing, very close to the Microsoft stand, and immediately I was into gear and said to him, "I'm sorry to interrupt you Mr Gates, have you got two seconds, I would love to interview you?"

He paused and then said, "Yes, how can I help you?" He went on to answer two of my questions but then he stopped and said "I haven't got time now, I have to appear on the Microsoft stand, but if you want any further help, here's the card of my personal assistant, a gentleman called John Pinette. Please get in touch with him and he will help you with anything else that you need."

I was delighted, and I don't know to this day if the questions I e-mailed through to John Pinette were actually answered by Bill Gates. I don't know, but what I do know is the first two answers came from him and the first question I asked him was "Are entrepreneurs born or can they be made?"

After a pensive thought he said, "Anybody can become an entrepreneur if they've got the passion and the will and the determination to succeed."

The second question was "How would you define success?" His answer was quite an enlightening one as well.
He said "Any person is only as successful as the people he or she surrounds themselves with."

I loved that answer. In my whole business structure this has become a very true statement, in that you'll only be successful if you've got good people around you, this is a key element of your success. Of course there is a lot more to it than that. As my story unfolds, I will share the nuggets that I've implemented to becoming **Wealthy and Happy.**

I thoroughly recommend investigative travel to anyone. If you can win a scholarship such as the Churchill Scholarship or any others that are available, it's a great way to change the direction in your life. I sincerely thank Dartington Cattle Breeding Trust (my scholarship sponsors) and Nuffield Farming

Scholarships Trust for affording me the opportunity of travelling and studying the topic of my choice.

Little did I know that as a result of embarking on this study that it would form the start of a speaking career. Incidentally the thought of speaking on stage was one of my biggest fears. I did not ever think I would be on stage speaking to people, however, with Nuffield Farming Scholarships Trust one of the remits is that you must speak for 20 minutes in front of a chosen audience within Nuffield on your topic study. There is a competition each year for the best presentation from all the Nuffield reports and talks with approximately 19 scholarships awarded each year.

When I heard about this and having been inspired by all the people I interviewed on my Nuffield tour, I was determined to win that award despite my fear of public speaking. This was a huge undertaking for me, I concentrated on the content of that 20 minute talk and I asked other leading speakers exactly how the content and delivery could be maximised in order to achieve the connection with the audience and reduce my fears. The common response from leading speakers was don't focus so much on the material, keep it extremely simple, be yourself on stage, be relaxed and don't try to be someone else. That was great advice. One of the key people who helped me with my speaking was a gentleman called Andy Harrington. I thank Andy for his input both then and now in helping me with my speaking career.

When I reflected on what Sir Richard said about being a 'lightworker' it dawned on me that at the end of the whole scholarship I knew exactly what that term meant as it had been raised a number of times during my tour. A number of leading entrepreneurs referred to myself and others who gave back and helped others as 'lightworkers'.

Something a little bit strange happened on the tour. When I arrived at Phoenix Arizona I was intending to interview a gentleman who is a change physiologist and he helped many sports people achieve great success. His name is Gary Mack and he lives on an Indian reserve on the edge of Phoenix Arizona.

I hired a car and drove towards Gary's house. There was a massive mountain to my left which 'disappeared' up into the haze. I couldn't actually see the top of it, which intrigued me. I have always loved mountains, I love walking them and I have always felt at peace during this pastime. After the interview with Gary Mack I had some time on my hands and decided to walk the mountain. I had a sports jacket on and some inappropriate shoes but I started walking anyway.

It was about mid-afternoon and as I walked on the lower paths of the mountain there were lots of people jogging and walking. After about an hour I started to get higher up the mountain where there were fewer people. It took me over three hours to walk to the summit, there was no-one there whatsoever and this was above the haze line of the red sky that was stretching right across Phoenix. Through the gaps in the red haze you could see the whole of Phoenix itself, what a wonderful sight. There was hardly any vegetation on top of the mountain and I sat on this massive grey rock looking out over this view, reflecting on what had been a brilliant journey as this was nearly the end of my Nuffield Scholarship Tour.

Squaw Peak, Arizona

As I was chilling out reflecting on life, I noticed a gentleman sitting to my right hand side and somehow he looked familiar. I wondered how he got there as I hadn't noticed anyone else walking up the mountain. Where had he appeared from I asked myself. He acknowledged me as he glanced in my direction. He was sitting about six metres away on another rock. After a few moments he looked across and said, "You know all those questions you are asking yourself, the answers are inside of you." It was profound. Bear in mind this was a total stranger who had appeared from nowhere as I sat on top of the mountain. That event coupled with the fact that, to my knowledge, I am of sound mind, and more than that, I was so determined to succeed in business that I hadn't touched any alcohol for at least a year prior to that moment. His words rung in my ears; I thought who are you? As I turned to ask him who he was, he'd gone, just disappeared. At that moment I wondered if I was just imagining things. Did I actually hear him? Was he really there? Yes he was there and yes that was what he said. I ended up running around looking to see where he had gone, it was as if he disappeared into thin air! Had he fallen off the mountain? Was he hiding behind a rock? I couldn't find him anywhere and that really perplexed me. I knew shortly after I had calmed down that it was my other spirit guide. I remembered Sir Richard referring to his spirit guides, it all made sense to me now.

When we were building our empire my daughter said to me when she was eleven years old "Dad, you're weird." I replied "Thanks babes." She often reminds me of that moment as we are very close. I feel you have to be a little bit 'different' as an entrepreneur in the way you do things. I wanted to be a business owner and to grow my own empire; all the seeds were now in place. A massive problem however that I possessed was a fear of failure, because I hadn't actually achieved any results. Even though I had the theory, it felt like this huge monkey on my back, I had to prove myself; I had to get on with it. I knew by this time what business I wanted to set up. The one area that really resonated with me, because it was simple and straightforward, was property. Many people I spoke with were either directly or indirectly involved in property investment, and the feeling and thought of buying a smelly, run down house and fixing it up and making it a nice home in which people could live resonated with me.

The key outcomes of my Nuffield Scholarship study were:

Entrepreneurs don't have to be born with certain genetics. Everyone has the possibility of achieving **Wealth and Happiness** if determined enough and they place themselves in the winning environment.

Successful people upskill themselves through knowledge gain.

Self-awareness is the master key to success. Knowing what we are good at, bad at and enjoy doing, is better self analysed by entrepreneurs.

Should you wish to download a free copy of my scholarship study report to see these results then it is available on my website www.kevingreen.co.uk.

Rich Rule 3

Press your start button

Many people wish to achieve **Wealth and Happiness** but are fearful of starting something in case they fail, initially I was no different. In order to learn about property investment and development I felt I needed to invest in myself and gain knowledge before going forward because it was an area in which I had limitations. I also realised that Sir Richard Branson was very interested in property and he referred to Necker Island not only as a lifestyle but as an investment. That struck a chord with me, realising that **Wealth and Happiness** could go hand in hand and property could bring that for me and my family.

My main reason for building an empire of any form was to provide security for my children and myself, having been homeless with no money whatsoever I value a sense of security, and more so financial security in putting food on the table for my children and looking after them like a good father should. As I started researching various property training organisations, I came across an American based training program. This had a whole structure of teachings that were being introduced to the UK, I decided to go along to a free two hour seminar on property investing and ended up paying for three days of training. On those three days of training, I bought further courses. They weren't cheap but the content was invaluable, I devoured the information and loved every part of it.

After I had completed my training I had the tool kit to buy my first house, which I did without using any of my own money.

So the scene was set. I was going to choose a house, I was going to make it work and I was going to strive forward. I met a mortgage broker who was very helpful and he highlighted the fact I needed deposit money from somewhere. I also needed some money for the refurbishments and for the legals. I had a plan; as long as he could get me the 85% loan to value mortgage then I could raise the deposit from credit cards. I didn't have any credit cards at that time; I never used or believed in them. I had a creative way to bridge the money using the credit limit on my credit cards, then I went to my aunty, who was kind enough to lend me some money for a period of time, she lent me eight thousand pounds to go towards the refurbs and the legals and I bought a property called Ty Canol in West Wales, a run-down little cottage and embarked on fixing it up. I carried out all the work myself apart from the gas and electrics where I had to engage the services of qualified professionals. Looking back it was perhaps a mistake doing the work myself as it slowed up the process.

My first house purchase, Ty Canol in South Wales (pictured after refurb works!)

I bought this property at discount and added value to it before refinancing the property to pay my aunty back and repay my credit cards. It was a pretty straightforward process, I had nothing to lose. I kept the property, rented it out, and retained a nice profit each month after all costs.

I really had the bug for property investment and I was still farming at the same time and to be fair to my wife, she was working hard on the farm therefore we decided to employ the services of a farm manager to help out and to ease the workload for both of us. I knew that by doing this I would be able to afford more time to pursue a career in property investment. The farm manger we employed was a lovely lad but didn't stay with us very long because my human resources management was terrible. I was interfering too much as I felt he wasn't running the farm exactly like I would run it! We were still living in the farmhouse, being on site just didn't work out and subsequently he left.

It was a tough time trying to run the property business and also run the dairy farm with the 400 milking cows.

The second manager was superb, we moved out of the farmhouse and it freed up our time.

The next house I purchased was bought in a similar way using creative financing, this time the intention was to sell for profit. In fact I did this twice in succession the first house made profit of £8,100. This time though I didn't do much work in it myself, I realised it had taken a long time to do the first one and it was going to be much quicker employing experts. Within a month the whole house was complete, new kitchen, new windows, new wiring, plastering, upgraded the bathroom and it looked really great. The outside of the house is equally important. The fence was painted and everything was neat and tidy. First impressions of buyers are vital and this one looked top notch.

I had been taught a system at the property trainings so I did it again with even less of my physical input in the third deal. This time there was a little bit more profit of £11,200. The strategy was building nicely, I now had a 'slush fund' of money and the profit was on reserve ready for the next deal, my property empire was gaining momentum. I was excited but I am so tight with my money that when I moved off the farm I lived in a rather large second hand mobile home which the kids were really excited about. By this time my ex-wife and I had agreed a 50/50 custody agreement of our children, and she moved into another property. The farm manager then continued to run the dairy farm without me looking over his shoulder.

Lessons Learned

The key focus when looking at growing a very lucrative business structure is to maintain control and ownership of that business. The true entrepreneurs are leaders and pioneers in their business sectors. Often times the biggest pay day for a business is when that business is sold and we need to be mindful of this when choosing a new business or growing an existing business structure. In my own example with properties being the main hub of business I maintain total control of the ownership. The properties are rented out and held outside of a company structure largely to allow me more flexibility on transfer of ownership into a trust for the benefit of my children; however, I have two profit centers from that portfolio.

The first is the income that the properties produce through the surplus rent i.e. the rent collected per month minus any expenses.

The second and often times the largest profit that is made on a property is when it's sold and it's capitalised.

Also, on the rented properties my net worth is also reflecting a very strong balance sheet when we look at the amount of equity that's held in total over the whole range of the numbers of properties that I now hold as one of UKs largest private sector landlords.

The person who controls the ownership of his/her businesses is generally the person who will make the most money for time invested.

The control element is also a typical personality trait of entrepreneurs, it brings us satisfaction that we haven't relied on direction from anyone else i.e. it could be the opposite of multi-level marketing and franchising where someone else is leading the way. We actually like being leaders, however, obviously it has its risks attached and business has to be thoroughly researched before implementation or start up. This is an area where I am extremely keen. I never get into any business area without fully knowing all the 'pros' and 'cons' of that business first and then deciding on the safest set up or growth structure for that particular sector.

It's always interested me that a good manager in business can have fantastic results and that the people we have in the business helping us are so important; this is often something that entrepreneurs get wrong. I've had my own challenges in growth structure but I'm happy to say the team that's on board today are superb. I'm very proud of all of them and their performance is excellent. The main objective for me is for my team to be happy and myself to be happy. I believe if we focus on just the money when starting up or growing businesses, money can actually run away from you. It's more important for everybody to enjoy what they do because you have chosen the business that suits your physiology; it gives you the wow factor.

Appointing the right people in the right areas is vital in growing a successful business.

A lot of potential millionaires will start out in business by themselves. I was exactly the same, we endeavour to possess a skill set in all areas in that situation, often times there are some pain barriers to go through as we realise we can't do certain things very well. I hate loads of paperwork and I remember the mess across my bedroom floor when I first started my businesses, it was a bit of a shambles to say the least. It taught me that systems and appointing the right people on your team are so important.

The businesses, whether it's a product or a service, should always be led by the market forces. With property we check the market demand, **we sell to demand and we rent to demand.** As time ticks by we then have to test and hedge against any market changes and the possible waning of public demand for that product or service.

I'm a huge fan of not putting all my 'eggs in one basket,' the risk factor when starting a business must be considered if we take notice of government statistics. They show us that businesses are more likely to fail than to thrive and quoting their statistics out of 100% of businesses that start up, by the end of year one only 20% have been successful. That is a huge drop off rate which only gets worse in year two and three.

The people that achieve **Wealth and Happiness** in business have put a lot of hard work and effort into it, usually not by physically being at the front end of the supply of that product or service but by planning, researching, controlling, appointing and creating superb clear structures for all to follow. In property, one of the key success principles for me in creating a massively successful and profitable business is the:

Three-Two-One Rule

For every **three** properties we purchase, I hold **two** and rent them out and I sell **one** for profit.

The profit that we make from the property that we trade, (the one we sell), is generally used to clear down debt of one of the two we hold as investment rentals. This has been an important action in my tool kit of growth for the property portfolio. In particular as we reduce debt on a rental property the amount of finance portion that has to be paid out from the rent reduces i.e. the total interest goes down as the capital debt is reduced and/or the capital payment has fallen because we are clearing debt which in turn pushes up cash flow. What I've done in my business is taken some of the cash flow profit to further pay down the debt. This approach to clearing debt down on the property portfolio created stability so that when the crash came in the property market, we were in a very strong position to buy more property as opposed to other investors who were too highly geared. In some cases those investors found themselves being repossessed by lenders because the debt on the properties was higher than the value of the assets.

The main safety aspect to consider when growing profitable business structures is 'not having all your eggs in one basket.' Ideally to have at least two business asset classes that we focus on. In my case when I started business the first asset class was property and property related business which included property lettings. We let and managed properties for other persons beside ourselves. However alongside property, in year one of start-up, I actively searched for another business start-up outside of property which was totally unconnected.

It's important to keep business simple.

In my property business I compiled a simple rule for growth for my buy to let portfolio which I call **The Rich Rules Financial Wheel** which allows me to regenerate my initial seed capital money to buy further investment properties. By flipping (buying and selling) deals and creating profit I managed to build up a 'slush' fund (savings) large enough to fully fund the cash purchase of my next deal. The way that **The Rich Rules Financial Wheel** works ensures that this slush fund is always replenished each time I place a mortgage on the property that I have already bought and refurbished to raise the property's value. An important tip on this action is:

It's easier to finance an asset I already own.

In the property business this means it's easier to obtain a mortgage when we already own the building as opposed to applying for a mortgage to purchase that same building.

See my simple flow chart on page 62 showing **The Rich Rules Financial Wheel.**

THE RICH RULES FINANCIAL WHEEL

FAIR MARKET VALUE 82K

SLUSH FUND
60k

Price =   50K
Legals & Refurbs = 5K
Total Spend =   55K

MORTGAGE

(82,000) X 75% = 61,500

In this **The Rich Rules Financial Wheel** example I bought a property for fifty thousand pounds, spent four thousand five hundred pounds on refurbishing it and a further five hundred pounds paying for legal conveyancing, therefore total spend is fifty five thousand pounds.

I knew that the fair market value (resale value) was eighty two thousand pounds through my market research and I had bought at a significant discount because it was initially 'cash' purchased using trusted techniques I had learnt on how to buy properties at discount.

I placed a mortgage on the property after refurbishment works were completed; therefore I mortgaged against the value not the purchase price. (N.B. some mortgage lenders insist you have the property in ownership for minimum periods of time which can be as long as six months before allowing a mortgage against fair market value.)

I then used the mortgage drawdown monies, in this case sixty one thousand pounds to repay into the slush fund. My objective is to always at least replenish the slush fund; in this case, I have not only replenished but repaid the fifty five thousand pounds owed and a further six thousand five hundred, so paid back sixty one thousand five hundred pounds.

This is a great rule as it allowed me to buy the next property using exactly the same **Rich Rule Financial Wheel**, in fact it's been one of the main rules that has helped me buy a huge number of properties in a relatively short time period and helps me massively in achieving **Wealth and Happiness.**

I also started a topsoil business where I bought soil and then sold it to customers for their gardens. It was pretty straightforward and call me sad, but I knew about soil because I'm an ex farmer! I knew what soil grows good grass; I knew the names of the soils. The best soil that we could source and sell was a 'red sandstone' which was free draining, provided good growth, and it was ideal for either 'taking' grass seed or to be covered by turf. Now the problem I had was I didn't have any significant spare funds to start that business and I remember mulling over how this was going to happen. I ran a regional newspaper advert to sell topsoil that I didn't have yet. I advertised topsoil at £12.00 a tonne, when the calls came in for the orders, my response was "I'm sorry we are out of stock at the moment, we have some more coming through, can I take your contact details and get back to you shortly when we have fresh stock?" This was a great way to test the market. The phone didn't stop ringing and I quickly realised I needed to source some soil to sell to these customers. Then almost immediately, when I was driving down the road, not too far away from where I lived, I passed this big heap of soil. It was red sandstone; it was surplus on a site where a commercial development was taking place. It looked like there was plenty spare. I turned into the site and spoke to one of the gents working on the project as a machine driver. He pointed me towards the project manager's office and I quickly scuttled over and had a chat with the project manager. I indicated that I would like to buy the heap of soil and he said he would find out with the company owner if this was possible. I asked if it would be in order for me to speak to the company owner myself and save him the hassle of negotiations as I've always been a strong believer that you have to speak to as high up the chain as you can get if you wish to achieve the best results. He phoned the owner of the business there and then and a meeting between us was quickly arranged.

When I met the owner of this heap of soil, who incidentally was a big time developer, he was quite sympathetic to my intentions. I didn't tell him initially that I didn't have the money to buy the soil; we first of all negotiated a price and estimated the amount of tonnage that was in the heap. There was roughly three thousand tonnes of soil there and he wanted it moved off site as soon as possible, in fact that was his priority. I already had a huge amount of orders and the next step that I engaged with was very creative. I now knew that he wanted that heap moved quickly and efficiently and I had planned to get a digger driver on site. I engaged the services of a haulage firm, charged the haulage and the digger loading costs to the customer and shipped the soil out to customers as quickly as possible. The fact that he wanted it moved quickly also gave me a negotiating tool and I suggested to the owner of the soil, namely, that I could move it quickly as long as he could consider payment terms. After some time in negotiation we agreed that I didn't need to pay for the soil up front, it was more important for it to be shifted quickly. It all had to be moved within thirty days by which time I needed to pay the three pound a tonne for the three thousand tonnes of top soil. We facilitated this by me signing a personal guarantee to the nine thousand pounds agreed. I knew I had the 'pipeline' order book for soil which I could go back to and I needed to move very, very fast if I was going to get that whole heap of soil shifted. The potential profit in that soil from paying three pound a tonne and selling at twelve pounds a tonne to the customer was gross profit before any other marketing costs etc. of nine pounds a tonne. The haulage costs and loading costs were being charged to the customer on top of the twelve pounds. The haulage of the soil was a very simple plan, the customers would pay depending on the amount of mileage they lived from this heap of soil and also it would get cheaper per tonne for them if they ordered more tonnage.

The scene was set, the deal was done and I was losing a couple of sleepless nights thinking 'if I don't move this quickly and pay for this soil then this could all turn to custard!'

I placed more adverts in local papers which were very close to the population centre of the heap of soil, the orders came flying in again and this, coupled with the database I already had, made it run sweetly, however it was a busy time.

I had to focus on getting that money in quickly so customers that paid cash had preference. In fact I realised that a lot of businesses on my Nuffield scholarship tour had failed because the product or service they had supplied wasn't paid for either quickly enough or was not paid for at all. In my system, I put a rule in place which was, the customers would either pay before the soil arrived, or on arrival but before the lorry driver had tipped the lever to tip the soil out from the lorry bed onto the customer's premises. Customers were quite within their rights to climb up the lorry bed steps and check the soil or just look at the samples in the bags that the lorry drivers had with them in their lorry. Then they had to pay the lorry driver cash on site. This turned out to be an extremely shrewd move and the monies came flooding in. What I didn't have at that time and perhaps I should have thought of it, was a facility to take credit and debit card payments. I was starting very small in the business and it is something I hadn't even considered the benefits of, quite different, however, in our businesses today.

We have in our office five different payment terminal machines for each business that can take credit and debit card payments either on site when we sign up tenants for rented accommodation, or when we provide other various products and services in each business which I'll describe later, plus we have the facility to take payments over the phone. That resulted in the collection of rent money through payment terminals in advance from the property business meaning much more rent was collected than had previously been the case on monies owed to us. The first year of having a payment terminal to collect rent owed saved us twenty three thousand pounds compared to the previous year's unpaid rent.

The top soil business was a hugely successful operation whereby half of that heap was shifted extremely quickly. Within ten days there had been one thousand five hundred tonnes sold and the rest was flying out the door. I'm a strong believer that integrity, delivering on time and sticking to your word in business are vital. I now had over nine thousand pounds in my hand and I decided that before the 30 days' time limit for payment, I would pay the previous owner of this heap of soil the monies as agreed, not on the 30 day period but at 14 days. I handed over the nine thousand pounds which he signed and receipted for and was absolutely delighted to be paid early on what for him was a problem solved. The soil was shifting quickly and a nice bit of income for him at the same time on what was a waste product surplus to his project requirements. That supplier subsequently went on to supply a huge amount of soil to us down the line, largely because he trusts my word and structure to deliver not only as agreed but often times even better than agreed.

The soil business is a typical example of taking someone else's waste and turning that into an asset that others will pay for. Later on in **The Rich Rules** I will suggest to you some business ideas relating to waste products that can turn a handsome profit. The second part to the top soil business was the ability to further sell products, what is termed an 'upsell' in business. When people buy soil, often times they will need turf, which is lawn turf. What I learnt from comparing farming to this trading business is:

People in primary production of any product or service often don't make as much money as the 'middle person.'

The 'middle person' is the person who buys or secures control on that product or service and sells it on again for profit. I have witnessed this as I've travelled the world. When customers started asking for lawn turf I decided that it would be better to source lawn turf from a third party supplier and if possible to get that supplier to send it direct to customer and possibly lay it for that customer also. If I could get a profit margin out of that transaction as well then there would be a three way benefit, our customer is happy to have the product or service they need at an affordable price, the supplier is happy because they don't have to spend on sales and marketing, all I'm doing is being an introducer as a 'middle person' business selling additional products and services to our customers (an upsell). What a fantastic outcome that was! We were making significant profits on lawn turf and we also decided to supply lawn seed where customers could plant their own lawn seed and grow their own lawns far more cheaply if they didn't need the grass straightaway.

I managed to find a wholesale supplier who would supply the lawn seed at a discount price and the lorry drivers would take the seed with them direct to the customer and deliver at the same time as the soil, another brilliant move!

The business then moved up a gear even more, we began to provide a consultancy service on the larger orders, one of our team would visit the site, estimate the amount of soil needed and advise the customer on the grade of soil, the amount of seed or lawn turf that might be required.

At this stage we realised a number of customers wanted screened top soil, very fine soil with no clods in it whatsoever, especially when they were looking at seeding the lawn themselves with lawn seed. Now this caused a dilemma for me because to buy a top soil screening machine that would add value to our business was going to cost a staggering £326,000.00 and this was a fairly new business start-up where I didn't have that kind of ready money. I mulled over how we were going to create screened soil from a normal heap of mixed soil but the answer didn't come from me. It came from the digger driver David. 'Dai The Digger' as he was called (all David's are called Dai in Wales) suggested that we could get the local blacksmith to weld up a hopper which was slightly wider than the front bucket of the digger with some mesh in the bottom of it with sizes that were big enough to allow the fine soil through but stop the clods and stones from going through. He would be able to screen the soil using the digger and the pallet forks on it to do the whole process. He suggested that if he tipped the soil into this hopper and there were some lumps left on top of the mesh, he could then use his pallet forks to tip the hopper over, empty out the lumps onto the ground, bash the lumps with the front bucket on the digger and pop them back through the hopper again, thus extracting more fine soil out of the lumps and separating the lumps from the rest of the stones in another heap. Well I could have hugged him because it was such a simple solution to the problem, and it sounded like it was going to work. We drew up a plan and went down to the blacksmiths, got a quote to build this hopper, it was £350.00. A very straightforward construction that was completed within a week, and it worked an absolute treat.

Regarding the consultancy service that we gave our customers, we now had three different grades of soil.

1. The mixed soil that we had always sold.
2. The screened top soil which we could charge double for i.e. £24.00 a tonne.
3. The stones and clods which could be placed in the base of the customers project for drainage, so we could sell that off as well. We put a price on that of £1.00 per tonne so even the waste material from the heap had a use for on-site projects.

We had created a niche within the business. The amount of profit on the screened soil was considerable. However when it came to the consultancy service for the customers we were saving them money because they only needed to put the final layer of soil onto their project as the screened soil. It was actually better to start with the clods at £1.00 a tonne if there was a lot of filling needed, then the mixed soil at £12.00 a tonne and top it with screened soil at £24.00 a tonne. We would sell them the seed as well to finish the project, a superb package. There were even cases where on a large soil order we would give the seed for free as a 'thank you' to the customer. The seed was not costing us a lot of money anyhow, by the time we had taken it from the big bags and bagged it into smaller bags, when we sold it there were big profits in that as well!

The business went from simply buying and selling a heap of soil, into grading soil, providing a consultancy service to the customer and engaging in a third party supply contract with lawn turf. The final step to that business was the supply of coloured stone and tree bark. A number of customers were landscaping and asking for these products. We had some regular customers who were landscape gardeners that we supplied soil to, they were looking for Cotswold stone or slate stone, so the next step for us was to price that up exactly as we had done with the lawn turf. We would get it delivered to the customer as a 'middle man' business. Exactly the same process for the tree bark for the borders, people wanted it so we could actually supply the complete package. It was great to have the feedback from our customers, happy customers, a quality product, an affordable product and service.

All the teams were happy also as it was a simple systemised operation where we didn't have to chase payments. The only chasing that was required was making sure that the third party suppliers delivered on time and as agreed. That was the only 'headache' that we really had in the business. One or two suppliers were dropped because they didn't deliver on time which reflected badly on us. It's the same in any business; you need to keep on top of that, as customers come first.

The way we grow or start a profitable business is important; it should be safe both financially and legally.

With the legislative requirements on the laws that govern our country one of the key learning outcomes for me that wasn't taught in school was the fact that I needed to get employers liability insurance very quickly if I was going to employ people. Even to this day, I am appalled at the fact that the basic legal requirements to a business start-up or growth are often not taught in school or in further education.

The topsoil business is a classic example of what I call the **peanut principle in business.** What do I mean by this? Well it's something I've termed to describe the business that doesn't need big capital to start it up and grows by using its own profits, i.e. this generic growth which is a very safe way to start and grow a business. We start with one 'peanut', i.e. buying and selling smaller amounts of soil which grows then into a whole bag of peanuts, buying and selling thousands of tonnes of soil, and providing all the additional services and products to that business for the customer's benefit.

The other main consideration with starting or growing a business is how you manage your time. What is your return on time invested in the business and that's what I term:

ROTI = **R**eturn **O**n **T**ime **I**nvested.

It's no good being in a business long term that robs hours and hours of your time because that just goes back to being like a job. In my view the word 'job' stands for 'just over broke' as that's generally where it keeps you! It's usually very bad for return on your time invested.

If we set up a business structure where we can maintain control and ownership and step back from that business while others provide the front line service and product to the customers, then we are being far more efficient with our own time.

In my own structure I am extremely careful with managing my own time. Today my personal assistant arranges meetings. I state the timings of those meetings like clockwork.

As I enter a meeting and engage with the person or people, I will immediately make it clear that I only have the 30 minutes or one hour, so that we get all negotiations completed quickly and on time. Should they not be completed by that time then further meeting may have to be arranged which tends to keep things tighter and more efficient. I'm also a lover of Apple's product iCal, the I calendar which collaborates all of the meetings and events throughout the day that my PA will have organised, and which I can see at a glance on my synced computer or i-Phone.

Being very strict on managing my time has led me to rely on other good people in the team and those people enjoy working in their various positions largely because they are rewarded well.

One of the tips that has helped me grow successfully is:

"I don't give away ownership of any business unless I really have to."

What I will do is give a profit share percentage of that business to the people who are helping to grow and increase those profits. I feel it is only fair, a great outcome of that is people who perform very well are well rewarded financially. It also has a direct benefit to me because as the business produces more profit then the value of that business goes up. When it comes to the time to sell or transfer that business then the benefit of that increase in value is realised.

Additional Tip:
Another key area I attribute my success to is the ability to network well with other people. It's not just what you know in business, it's who you know, and sometimes those introductions have to be strategically planned.

We are only 3 steps away from any person that we need to speak to, and if we really intend and focus hard on meeting that person anything is possible.

If I'm in an environment where I meet people who could be mutually beneficial to work with, I will exchange business cards and I'll always follow up quickly with that person. Within 24 hours of meeting them, either directly by myself or via my PA, a message will be sent simply saying it was great or lovely to meet them, and look forward to speaking again shortly.

Entrepreneurs don't like long and lengthy stories in emails and messages; we prefer it to be short, sharp and to the point. I recognise this when I am engaging with other entrepreneurs, so the message is always kept brief, simple and clear.

If I am meeting a new person I will only move forward in business with that person if I can feel a rapport being created. I think to myself 'would I like to spend some time this evening relaxing and having a chat with this person, would I enjoy their company?' If the answer is yes then I can feel that rapport. If the answer is no, I will always send a message to that person that it was nice to meet them but won't engage in any form of joint venture.

If you haven't got rapport with the people you are dealing with, then somewhere down the line it is highly likely to come round and 'bite you in the bottom.'

We have all heard that planning and goal setting is so important and that is so very true, it is one of the most basic fundamentals to setting up the right business framework. If you do not set clear goals, how are you going to relay clearly what your intentions for that business are to your team?

We must set these targets and goals, and we must believe and know that we can achieve these goals. Once the goals have been set the action plan to achieving those goals needs to be thoroughly considered and written down on a piece by piece basis. The way that I have started and grown businesses and continue to do so is again a very simple approach. It consists of minutes and action plans where I hold myself accountable all the way through the journey to achieving each particular goal.

So an entrepreneur like myself doesn't naturally like writing a lot of stuff down, but we have to get over that and keep a record of our progress containing the actions to achieving the end results, then hold ourselves accountable to those actions. We can quickly see if we are going off track using this process and consider how that can be remedied to get back on track.

I am also a strong supporter of:

"Success is the journey not the destination" John Wooden

What this means is if we focus only on our goals and we only view achieving them as success, then sometimes the journey to achieving them can be a sad journey or something we don't enjoy, and that usually means we are in the **WRONG** business.

The other great thing about business is that we never do achieve our ultimate goals. As we move towards our goal and make our goal a success, we might be a little bit perturbed, for we don't ever achieve our ultimate goals because we keep moving them forward. I have included a planner on page 89 for you to use which will help you plan your goals and actions and hold yourself accountable as you start and grow your own businesses.

Goal Setting

Goal setting is the key to any business plan.

Goals must be **S.M.A.R.T.E.R.**

*S*pecific

*M*easurable

*A*ttainable

*R*ealistic

*T*imely

*E*valuated

*R*ecorded

*S*pecific

Define your expectations. You need to be specific, for example in 5 years' time I want to have purchased 100 properties for my portfolio.
Not "one day I might buy another property".

*M*easurable

Quality, quantity, timeliness and cost. Goals must be clearly set out so that everyone would agree whether the performance criteria was met or not within the stated time scales.

*A*ttainable

Challenging goals within reason. Do not assign too many goals even though each one is within reason.

Consider:-
- Past performance
- Available resources
- Experience
- Motivation

*R*ealistic

Link the goal to higher level business unit goals. If goals are set at an unrealistically high level they will be ignored and demotivating.

Timely

Make a diary note for completion of the goal.

Evaluated

Evaluate goals regularly and adjust them as needed to account for changes in finance or availability of resources.

Recorded

Keep clear records of all progress, we use action plans at all stages which we review on a weekly basis to hold ourselves accountable.

Action Planner

Goal:

Objective:

Major Actions	Target Completion Date	Actual Completion Date	*Targeted Performance	*Actual Performance

Define how you will measure success of an objective in a way that means something or makes sense to you i.e. Scale out of 5 where 1 is not achieved in the time frame and 3 is achieved to timescale and 5 is exceeded objective before deadline.

The next step is quite straightforward when we are looking at starting or growing a business, sometimes it is easier to investigate what the competitors are doing and do something similar or better!

It is often said there are very few new things on this planet, and we can find the answers we need by searching within the existing knowledge structures. Often the best way to approach this is to become a customer of the potential competitor's product or service, so you can gain the customer experience and learn from the good points and bad points. Ask yourself 'how do they treat their customers?'

We have to consider intellectual property rights, trademarks and patents and be sure we don't fall foul of any of them. When we set up our own business and structure, we trademark the business name and logo, be sure to do the same. If we need a patent we get that in place too, because this will create more business value and protection for ourselves.

The planning and actions are carried out on an ongoing basis, and this is achieved in my world by allocating what I like to call 'chill out time' every day.

It consists of me having at least half an hour of time to myself, where the mobile phone goes off and there are no other interruptions. For instance if I am at home in my house on the hill in Wales, we have three hammocks slung across the A-Frames of the vaulted ceiling and I will use one of them to relax. It is a house that I renovated myself, and it's a lovely family place to live with our bedrooms downstairs and the lounge, kitchen utilities and other living areas upstairs.

Pictured on page 92 is the hammock in my lounge, it overlooks the sea. I love to lie here during my chill out time.

There are no other properties close to my house; it's a very serene and quiet area. This is where I ask myself:

Are my kids ok? Is there anything I need to change? Is there any way that I can help or empower them? Are my businesses on track? What needs to be tweaked? What new ideas should I consider going forward?
Are we all happy?

It's one of the most productive times of the day for me. I don't know whether you have noticed this but as you are waking from your sleep in the morning or you are going off to sleep at night, it's quite often the time when the ideas flow. This is replicated for me while I'm lying in my hammock .Chill out time, or meditation as some people call it, helps the creative juices flow. If I am not at home in Wales, the other places I love to chill out are on top of a mountain or hill – I may be driving my car and I will pull over, tilt the driving seat back slightly, half close my eyes, and have some "me" time.

$\mathcal{R}$ich $\mathcal{R}$ule 4

Embrace Change

Change is powerful

Two years post my decision to go 'full on' into property, we decided to sell all the dairy cows and sell the milk quota (an allowance to produce milk which used to have a good value). It was an easy decision to make in the end, because the increased cow numbers had pushed up farm profits, but more importantly had increased the allowance for a payment from the Government whereby we would be paid by the European fund for not producing milk!

Ironic as it seems, farmers at that time could get paid for the milk they had produced in previous years and receive a bigger payment when they stopped producing milk. So we pushed up the cow numbers and pushed the milk volume for the period of time to qualify for that. It was a strategic business decision and the objective was to then clear the debts on the farm.

We subsequently cleared all debts from the sale of cows and the milk quota then rented the farm out.

This was a joint decision by the family. When we sat down and put all the figures together, it made sense. The net result was that the income achieved from renting out and the Government grant was nearly matching the net profit that could be made by continuing with farming!

The major bonus with this option was I got all of my time back, I had been putting a lot of time into the farm whilst also growing the property business, and it was really full on. The fact that we could get our time back and with that, a lot more happiness, was very important.

The Government would continue to pay grant based subsidy for a further 10 years, so this was a long-term strategic decision. Also it was better not to sell the farm because land and property does go up a lot in value and more importantly our children may wish to go into farming further down the line. It would have been selfish to sell the farm, should that have been the case. So the option was kept open for their future.

My parents were very happy, as the main owners of

the farm, the debts were cleared and it was still making good profits.

Sometimes when you're in farming or front-line business, you don't look at the bigger picture, but taking time to step back and look at the overall outcome confirmed renting the farm was certainly a very sensible option. I was still relying on only five hours sleep a night; this meant I could get a lot more free time as well. One thing I focused on was quality time with my children. Getting 'unmarried' went relatively smoothly; the split custody of our children remains to this day and has worked extremely well for all of us.

My Mother and Father were very; very helpful all the way through, helping with our children should they need the odd lift from school or dropping off at football etc. or any other events that took place. I dearly thank them for all their help. As usual it was all hands-on and my father started becoming very interested in the property side of things. I noticed quite a difference in him, in particular in his approach to everything that was happening at this time.

When I first went into property remember my

Father called the property business "that property thingy" and I don't think he fully thought it would be quite as successful as it turned out to be, but he supported me all the same, he was keeping an eye on what I was doing.

The biggest change came around this time from my Father as he'd retired from farming and was really at a bit of a loose end. He'd also had an endowment pay-out where he had paid £28,000 into an endowment policy over 10 years roughly, and the maturity sum that he had back was £32,000. So he paid in £28,000, he had back £32,000 over 10 years and at that time Mother and Father could notice that it hadn't even really kept pace with inflation, it was a relatively poor pay out.

I'm not a strong supporter of pensions, TESSA's, ISA's or PEP's because somebody else is controlling your money. I've always been able to do a far better job controlling money myself and cutting out the middleman.

It was at this point that my father approached me and he said "This property thingy, tell me a bit more about it and tell me if I'd have put my £28,000 investment into the property thingy like you do it, what would be the minimum outcome of **Wealth** that I'd have right now?" We worked out using my three-two-one principal and some yield calculations and returns on investment that I'm about to show you in **The Rich Rules** and what Father would have had back minimum was one and a quarter million pounds for his £28,000 investment over that 10 years!

Father could hardly believe the figures, he was like "WOW, why didn't someone tell me this before?" So Father said "Right this £32,000, I'm putting it straight into property, will you help me out?" I said, "Willingly, I'd love to."

He said, "I want to grow this £32,000 into something bigger but I want to control it myself this time and then it will benefit the grandchildren." I said "Absolutely, what a great idea." He said, "I'm going to use the money to put a deposit on a property and go and get a mortgage." I said, "Brilliant Father, but there is one thing to consider." I explained to him that if he wished to continue getting mortgages there should be a different approach.

It's the same for anybody; this is something I've

taught myself. The banks look at one's ability to clear debt from a mortgage, so it's important to clear a capital sum regularly to help with approvals for future borrowings.

This is what is called in the trade 'capital adequacy' and it forms part of our credit profile. When a person can prove to the lenders that they can clear capital debt on a regular basis, they are more likely to be able to borrow money to go to the next venture. That's quite the opposite of people who borrow money and just pay the interest on it and do not clear any capital debt. What happens in that case is that particular investor would reach 'saturation point' where he or she would be seen by the main banks as too high risk to be lent to. It's far better to follow the rule of the game that I put in place which is a three-two-one principal, where we trade at least one third of our business assets and then take the profit from that trade and start paying down some of that capital debt on the two properties we keep as investments.

My Father understood this principle very quickly and I explained that in order to create a debt and clear that debt, the quickest way that he could do this (and this is what I've learned from my Robert

Kiyosaki trainings) is to take a credit card or two in his name, use that money to fund the deposit of the property, and then use the property profits to clear the credit cards. That will create good capital adequacy, a good credit profile and start proving to the lenders that were subsequently going to lend to my father that he was a sure bet.

The other benefit of creating a debt and then clearing it is that your credit score gets stronger. Obviously a word of warning here, if you are using the route through credit cards, they can be a great tool if you know what you are doing, but a very, very destructive tool if you don't.

I've used this approach quite extensively in the way that I've built up my property portfolio, and my Father could see the sense in it after a while. He didn't initially believe in creating debt as he'd always been taught that you have to get a job and earn money before you buy anything, and of course this is a total reversal of that thinking. Now let's go back to leverage and gearing and how other people's money can work for you.

Father sorted out an undervalue deal, a stinky, smelly property, put the deposit on the credit cards, got a buy to let mortgage, fixed the property up, refinanced it and paid off the credit cards and paid off the original loan.

My Mother was full of joy and **happiness** to see my father so excited about his new venture. He had just become a property investor. It was fantastic for me to witness as well because when you can inspire and empower a close family member, I think that's quite special.

Father had a brilliant remit that was very similar to mine, where he wanted to create security for his grandchildren and that was his reason for doing what he was doing. At the same time he loved it. Father's objective was to buy a handful of properties using the three-two-one rule and follow exactly the systems that we'd put in place.

Father is very frugal and he was watching those numbers very carefully. I remember the only funny side of it all was that Father was so hands on in the beginning he would be meddling with the refurbishments and doing the work himself, much as I did with my first couple of properties. The builders were saying "Go away Alan, leave us to it, we know what we're doing." And of course it's very difficult not to get involved with things when you think you can do it perhaps better than somebody else.

The whole bigger picture today, Father now has a number of rental properties and he's a very happy bunny, and that means a huge amount to me in that my Mother and Father have achieved **Wealth and Happiness** and they are both a lot healthier for it.

I think when you love what you do, there are side benefits and better health is one of them.

After exiting frontline farming, there was a new lease of life for me as well. I went absolutely flat out on building my property portfolio. It was all in my name now the divorce settlement and decree absolute had come through. The financial statement had been put in place and everything with my ex-wife was fine, and that was a big relief for me, knowing that everybody was happy. After all the hard work and strife and dedication, it was starting to really pay off now.

The one keepsake from my farming career is my pet donkeys. There is an interesting story aside; I had a joyous moment when farming when I was buying extra cows during the time I was increasing the cow numbers. I went to a farm sale and unbelievably this sale was held in a town in South Wales named Bethlehem! There was a small herd of cows being sold which were ideal for our grazing system at that time. I intended to buy quite a few from the sale, in fact they were a good value purchase and I ended up buying nearly half the cattle there on that day.

As the sale came to an end between the auctioneers and the old farmer who was retiring, the old farmer came up to me and said "Thank you for buying those cows and I know they are going to a good home, but I've got one concern. That cow over there (and he pointed to the cow), one of those you bought, is Primrose. Primrose has a friend and the friend is a donkey." He explained that he would really like me to buy the donkey so she could remain friends with the cow, and if I didn't it was highly likely that the cow and the donkey would pine for each other and become ill. I was intrigued by this and I followed the farmer around to the back of the farm, to this old stone barn.

You know you get those moments where you think

this is so surreal, as we came around to the barn, there was a hole in the wall where the window should have been and it was all tumbled down, but through this hole there was a shaft of sunlight shining through into this old stone barn. In the middle of the barn was this donkey, a cute, fluffy little donkey and this shaft of sunlight was shining straight onto the donkey's withers. Right on the top of her back I could see a clear dark cross, the colour of this cross was clearly evident across its shoulders. I raised this with the farmer. "Oh yes," he said, "folklore has it that when Jesus was crucified on the cross, the donkey that carried the heavy cross was left with a mark across his withers, and ever since then pure bred donkeys have carried this 'cross' mark." This donkey then turned around and looked at me as if to say 'please take me home with Primrose the cow' and so there and then I struck a deal with the farmer to take this donkey back to the home farm.

The donkey had no name; it was quite a young Jenny donkey which is a female donkey.

When I took the donkey back and introduced her to Primrose again, the delight was evident from both of them. They were bouncing around like little

Bambi's delighted to see each other. Then the donkey proceeded to go and introduce herself to the other 400+ cows that were in the dairy herd and it was quite a delight to see the respect that these cows gave her.

The donkey was half the size of the cows but she was clearly in charge, and within a week she was the leader of the whole herd without any doubt whatsoever. The donkey was so fast on her feet that if a cow tried to tackle her or fight her she always gained the upper hand. The donkey would spin round, give the cow a good kick with her back legs and then the cow would show respect back to the donkey.

My children immediately fell in love with the donkey, she was so friendly and fluffy, and she craved the attention, a real pet. My children had to think of a name for the donkey and at the time the Spice Girls were big and they came up with the name Victoria, named after Posh Spice. My children loved to feed Victoria carrots and biscuits and really fussed over her. The great thing for me with farming was whenever we needed to move the cattle we just called Victoria and the whole herd would follow her. One of our neighbours, who was also a dairy farmer, noticed this and proceeded to buy a donkey for his own milking herd, and exactly the same thing happened there!

Donkeys naturally lead dairy cows, I'd never heard of this before, but since then I've now heard it said many times.

Unbeknown to me, the outcome of this story is a bit special, because Victoria was in foal. Some three months later she had a female Jenny foal and the children named that foal Emma, again after the Spice Girls. I've still got Victoria and Emma today. When I left dairy farming I took them to where I live now, they have continued breeding and we now have fifteen!

The outcome being is that I'm very, very fond of my donkeys and they keep me very grounded.

Emma and Victoria are in the middle!

Calculations

I'd like to take you back to the **Rich Rules** through the key calculations that I use when I'm looking at property deals and some clear profit margin benchmark figures that we look at for all businesses.

The first calculation that I look at when considering purchasing a property is the yield calculation. The yield is calculated by taking the annual gross rent, dividing that by the property purchase price and multiplying that by one hundred over one to express it as a percentage.

You will see the calculation laid out as follows:-

Property Gross Yield

$$\frac{\text{Annual Gross Rent}}{\text{Property Price}} \quad x \quad \frac{100}{1}$$

$$= \quad \%$$

I have a benchmark for the minimum yield that I will accept. The minimum yield is very easy to

The
Rich
Rules
Steps to
Wealth &
Happiness

calculate in my world, when you understand it.

I check what the interest rate is on the mortgage I would need to buy the property; I make sure the minimum yield is at least four points higher than the mortgage interest rate.

Take a look at the following example to simply explain:

If I have an interest rate of 6% on a mortgage, 6% + 4 which is the four points margin that I need for my yield equals 10%, so I would want my yield calculation to show at least 10% yield on a property before I buy it.

It's a good indicator of the cash flow that property can produce for me. The reason that I look for that margin is I have other costs and void periods (empty days) on the property which I need to cover to make sure that it's as low risk as possible. Even if I'm buying a property with the intention of selling it to satisfy the three-two-one rule, I make sure that I get the yield calculation covered because should I not be able to sell a property, I can always revert to the exit strategy of renting it out and knowing that it 'washes his face'.

This is a term we use when the property produces enough income to more than pay for itself and put money in my pocket.

The second calculation I look at is cash flow. Cash flow is calculated on a monthly basis and is laid out as follows:-

Basic Cash Flow Calculation Table

(Per Calendar Month Basis)

(+) Rent	10%
(-) Mortgage Interest	?
(-) Lettings & Management fee	10%
(-) Buildings Insurance	
(-) Certificates	10%
(-) Repairs & Maintenance	

Total =

The cash flow required would need to be a surplus on the bottom side. The minimum surplus I look for on property in the UK would be £100 per month margin ideally; after all other costs are paid for. You can see in the table above we've got the

The Rich Rules

Steps to
Wealth &
Happiness

gross rent coming in, a figure per month.
Then we've got the mortgage interest rate, we have
an interest only mortgage on this particular
example and we have allowed 10% for letting and
management fee as a deduction and 10% for all
other costs.

N.B. All other costs include certificates for a
property (which consist of a gas safety certificate,
an electrical safety certificate and an energy
performance certificate, these legal requirements
are for the UK) and repairs and maintenance.

If we refer back to the three certificates first of all,
in the UK the gas safety certificate must be
renewed annually or at tenant changeover, the
electrical safety certificate is once every five years,
unless it's a PAT test for white goods and then
that's every year after the first year from new.

The energy performance certificate, which
measures the energy efficiency of a property, is
once every 10 years. So those together with repairs
and maintenance form roughly 10% of gross rent
when we are doing our first round deductions.

As you can see by the table on page 110 for this

example, if we take away the interest rate, the letting and management fee, and all other costs from the rent, we are left with a margin, and remember that margin for me must be at least £100 per property per month. Of course that doesn't work everywhere. There are only certain property types in certain areas where we can get these kinds of cash flow margins, and that's the type of property that I buy and put into my portfolio.

The next calculation is a capital calculation and this is calculated on an annual basis. The whole of the industry uses what's called return on investment (ROI).

Return on investment is calculated as follows:-

Return on Investment (R.O.I)

$$\frac{\text{Annual Gross Rent}}{\text{Deposit}} \times \frac{100}{1}$$

$$= \quad \%$$

Annual gross rent comes in divided by the deposit

that's required to purchase a property, and it's the annual gross rent divided by the property deposit x 100 over 1 to express it again as a percentage.

The reason that the property industry does this is it wants to calculate the yield return on the deposit invested, so the return on your own money. Now although it's a good guide as a calculation, I do have a problem with this because I know as a well-established investor that we have to put more money in than just the deposit when we are setting up a property. For instance the capital that I would have to find, to go alongside a mortgage if I want to buy a property, would be not only the deposit money but also money for the legals, and the refurbishments on a property, and if there is any property sourcing fee, or any other miscellaneous costs that I have to find, it would also have to be factored in.

So I've calculated an updated version of the return on investment and I've called it the **True Rate of Return** because it does reflect the true capital yield on your money invested after all capital is included.

This table is as follows:-

True Rate of Return (T.R.R)

$$\frac{\text{Annual Gross Rent}}{\text{All Capital Invested*}} \times \frac{100}{1}$$

$$= \qquad \%$$

* includes:

Deposit
Refurbs
Legals
Sourcing fee
Miscellaneous

The topside is similar to return on investment, we have got the annual gross rent but on the bottom side now included is all the capital added together, and then we express it as a percentage 100 over 1 again. So we divide the whole of the capital into the annual gross rent to get to our percentage figure, which gives me a true reflection of the return of my deposit invested.

Like the initial yield calculation when we are checking the cash flow of a property what I'd like as a margin for my **True Rate of Return** on investment, is again a four points margin over the mortgage interest rate.

So it's easy to remember, whatever the interest rate is for a mortgage on a property, even if you buy the property in cash, I would consider that I am actually borrowing money at the normal rate from time to time, what that money would cost, and I would then put four points above it.

Like the previous example, but this time let's take a slightly different interest rate of 5%. If the interest was 5% on this particular property deal, add four points onto that which would mean I'd need to show a minimum true rate of return at 5+4 = 9% then that shows me my money is working fairly hard for me, remember that's just the ingoing calculation.

If properly goes up in value then that's an added bonus, but we don't buy for definite capital growth, however, we are buying equity by buying at a discount initially, then running through those main three calculations of yield, cash flow and true rate of return.

Just in case you are finding that this is a little bit difficult to understand, I have prepared some software to help you which does it all for you!

You can access this complementary software from me by returning the FREEPOST slip at the back of **The Rich Rules** with your contact details and we will send it to you.

Using these simple strategies I became a millionaire 18 months after beginning my quest for **Wealth and Happiness**.

I used to visualise sitting on a beach in Barbados by St Lawrence Gap; I had seen pictures of it many times in the holiday brochures.

My wish was to be sitting on that beach enjoying the Caribbean weather, with a Mojito cocktail in my hand, knowing the money was coming in without me having to work at the frontline for it. That's what true passive wealth means to me.

18 months after I started my property business, there I was, I was doing exactly that, sitting on the beach in Barbados living the dream. It was fantastic!

I feel that when you are working really hard, don't ever forget to reward yourself, but only reward

yourself with what you can afford each time.
That was a real benchmark for me, patting myself
on the back and saying "Kevin, the hard work is
now paying off". I did get a little bit bored I can tell
you, on the beach, it was not something that I
wanted to do for the rest of my life. I found
business exciting, I wanted to continue and I started
diversifying. I think sometimes when you travel and
you have a holiday, you come back to the business
and 'hit it' even harder because going away from
your business ensures that you chill out for long
periods of time, and that's when more ideas start
flowing and you can't wait to get back 'on it'.

That's exactly how I felt, so the next stage was set. I
knew that if I went into another business, I could
buy something and sell it for profit. I would
consider how much margin I would want before
going into that business. The first benchmark that I
put in place was that I would accept a minimum of
20% net profit on any trading proposal going
forward, but most importantly I had to have a
passion for that business. I had been in dairy farming
and I didn't enjoy it, so I pledged to myself going
forward that,
"I'm going to enjoy every second of the day."

I needed to buy a second-hand mobile home again after moving from the dairy farm to where I live now. Being tight I shopped around to see where to get the best bargain, rather than buy from the traders I went straight back to source. There was a Haven holiday camp very close to where I originally lived on the farm in West Wales. I made some enquiries and found that each year they disposed of fairly new stock in order to upgrade. I found that I could buy not only one mobile home for myself, but a whole group of them and possibly sell them on for profit.

So before I agreed to any negotiations with Haven I quickly researched the market place to see what price I could immediately sell these mobile homes on for. In this short time frame I found the Southern Irish market would pay the most money for them. I found a contact there who wanted to buy the whole lot from me.

I actually achieved 35% profit margin on each mobile home. All I had to do was get them transported from the Haven site in West Wales onto the ferry in Pembroke Dock and that was a no-brainer for me.

It not only meant that the mobile home I bought was free, financed from the profit of the others, but it also meant that I had a significant few grand in my pocket for my time. So that became a new business for me. I was buying and selling mobile homes and I loved it because the return of time invested was brilliant and it was a nice, straightforward, simple business. I didn't need a lot of capital for that one; I just needed some good contacts, a good transport haulier and some people who would deliver on time.

Two of the second hand mobile homes I bought from the holiday camp and rented out as holiday lets on our farm.

Another business which I still do today is buying and selling motorway barriers. It evolved through the knowledge in my farming background. When I was building a new milking shed for the cows some years ago, to cope with the increasing cow numbers, I found that the most cost effective way to put railings on a yard which were cow friendly was to buy second-hand motorway barriers, those galvanised barriers that you see on the side of the road.

I managed to buy quite a few of them, in fact I bought a whole lorry load even though I didn't need the full amount myself. At the time I managed to buy them for scrap value when metal was weighing in at around a hundred and ten pounds a tonne for that type of metal and it worked out to around three pounds a barrier in scrap value.

Not every barrier was perfectly straight or in perfectly good order. There were the odd handful that maybe were a little bit rusty or had a bend or dent in them. I pulled those bad ones out of the load and I sold those ones back into scrap for the same price that I bought them for, and then I used the barriers I wanted myself. The surplus, which was about two thirds of the load, was sold to other farmers in smaller lots. I had paid three pounds a length for them but actually sold at £13 a length, so I had gross profit there of £10 on each one!

It was an absolute no-brainer, the farmers to this day love using them because the motorway barriers are predrilled every six-foot to match up to a post. Farmers build cattle handling pens, they build walls on yards and buildings, and they'll last for 'donkeys' years. So it's a very, very sustainable business.

Also the law change in the UK on health and safety fell into my favour because the Government decreed that motorway barriers are not as safe as concrete pillars. That led to the UK barriers being replaced by concrete shuttered walls down through the central reservation. You may have seen these tapered walls as you drive around. The remit by the Government is to get them all changed within the next 20 years. So I know this business has a 20 year life span. I am quite happy to continue buying second-hand motorway barriers from the motorways and ship them direct to farmers!

Another very simple business, often the profit can come from the simplest form of buying and selling. Two businesses that have been very lucrative with us and are still running today are:-

1. The property lettings business, where we charge 8% for full property letting and management to third-party landlords.

This is of course something we know very well, using our own resources.

2. Property sourcing. Some people, especially overseas buyers, wish to buy property through us because we know the business very well. We package the whole deal so that it's a passive investment for them, and this has become a major business.

It's something any one of you could do. A lot of Russians, Chinese and Asian buyers are particularly looking for property in the UK. It is seen as a very sound investment with a safer currency.

Later in **The Rich Rules** I'll list examples of simple profitable businesses that you can start.

One of my dreams was to live in a house on a hill with no neighbours, I wanted a house with sea views as I've always loved water. A long private driveway up to the holding and this driveway would be tree-lined. I could picture it very clearly in my mind. I mentioned this dream to my healer friend, Sandie, and her response was:

"If you intend strongly enough your vision will become a reality."

I intended strongly that this dream would be realised and within seven months of that initial intention, I heard of a property that was coming up for sale. The person that owned it had a big tax bill to pay, which I fully understand. Allegedly what this person had done was build houses, moved into them and claimed the principal private residence relief, which means when he sold the house he wouldn't have to pay any capital gains tax on it because it was treated as his home. He then moved on and built and lived in the next one, and the one after that.

The Inland Revenue had apparently said to this gentleman that he was trading and intentionally avoiding capital gains tax and apparently they slapped on a £95,000 tax bill on him. Through my business networking I heard that this gentleman who had the bill to pay, owned a holding, and by this time I was getting very interested in not only property investment and property trading but also land development. My next plan was to buy farms, gain planning permission on old barns and then sell them on for profit. I was very interested in what I heard regarding the holding he owned as there were old barns and a tumbledown house on the property. It was apparently in a nice position, but it hadn't dawned on me that this might be the dream home that I had been wishing for.

I went and had a look at the holding and as I drove up the driveway to this lovely serene setting, overlooking the sea with this tumbledown old house, I realised this was my dream home! The only thing missing was the tree-lined driveway. I thought that can easily be put right, I can plant some. The house, even though extensive works were needed on it, was in the perfect position and I felt that I could gain planning permission to extend it.

Plus there were some old barns on the holding, it had huge potential. I got very excited!

I quickly found the gentleman that owned it and although it wasn't officially for sale. I said "That tax bill you've got, that your associate told me about, would you like some help in paying that?"
He replied "Yes please."
I said, "Well I'm interested in a property that you own, would you consider then, in lieu of payment for your tax that you sell me the holding?"

"No." he replied
"No worries whatsoever," I said, "I can move quickly on this and should you wish to come back at any time please don't hesitate to contact me. Thank you for your time and your trouble." I departed after leaving my contact details.

Sometimes if you force a deal it pushes people away, so I'd 'left the door open' for him to come back to me any time.

Within a week the phone was ringing, he'd received some final demand for the payment of the tax and he was sounding fairly desperate. He said, "Look if you move fast and you put this money into my account straight away, I will sell you the farm and small holding. I have to pay this bill."
We met and the deal was done. That's how I bought where I now live and I was really excited. It was hard to find the money to buy it and I scrimped and gathered everything together as my assets were mostly 'tied up' in property deals.

But I managed it. I had to, because I had my dream to buy this place! The next thing was to get the planning permission sorted. That was a real headache, because I knew this was in a site of special scientific interest, what's called an SSSI, through the knowledge I gained through my land development training. Applying for planning for extensions or change of use on buildings can be an extremely difficult process.

Due to some ramblers spotting a marsh fritillary butterfly in the woods near the house, they reported this to the local authorities some years prior. The habitat of the butterfly species was found in the woods, so in order to protect this rare breed, the council had designated the area a site of special scientific interest.

This had both positive and negative aspects, the negative being, it is very difficult to obtain planning permission in those areas, but on the positive side nobody else would build anywhere near me because it was so isolated and the whole hill is protected by an SSSI. As nobody else would be able to build nearby, I felt for sure my privacy would be maintained on the holding. I was confident that there wouldn't be any development allowed in future years on this greenbelt, especially with an SSSI being in place as well.

It took me 14 months to gain planning consent for

the extension but I achieved it. That's the only holding in recent years that I've worked on physically myself, and I enjoy working there. Interestingly something great happened when a gentleman came to do the sand blasting, to enhance the old stone that was on the house. He was one of these 'weird' people like me and he said, "I'm into ley lines." I'm quite open to anything like this. He said "The reason the feeling of this house is so good is because outside the front door of this property, you have five ley lines crossing". That made sense to me because after I'm away on very intensive business meetings and then I return home, it feels so serene.

Most cultures have traditions and words describing the straight, often geometric alignments know as ley lines that run across ancient landscapes, connecting both natural and sacred prehistoric structures together.

So that kind of science and information interests me, it never used to but as a result of travel it makes you more aware that there is something greater than us out there.

I am a big believer in the **law of intention**. It

absolutely works a treat! It's worked many, many times for me, if you have true intent from your heart. That was a classic example that the universe will deliver for you. The best thing about our home is it's a beautiful place to bring up my children. A close friend of mine enhanced the whole experience. My daughter loves dolphins and my friend Jane is an artist, and she painted a shoal of dolphins on Llinos's bedroom wall, it's a brilliant painting.

Jane painted for my two sons also. My youngest, Emyr, loves machines and so he got a big track machine with the name Emyr on the boom, and then my middle child, Carwyn, loves motorbikes so she painted him on a big scrambling bike, jumping with the front wheel in the air on the wall. It's those little touches that enhance a lovely home for my children. The added benefit has been the safety. As they grew up they were away from the main roads and they could enjoy themselves in the woods and the countryside around.

Benefits of Wealth and Happiness.

One of the biggest benefits of becoming financially secure for me is the ability not only to provide security for my children but also a very good private education for them. I have mild dyslexia and it wasn't diagnosed until the later years of my life so I didn't get on very well in school. My academic ability is very poor, although I think people who suffer with any form of dyslexia and/or autism, and are on the spectrum, are brilliant in many other ways.

I don't feel that academic ability is directly linked to intelligence. What we found with my oldest son, Carwyn, (he is like a mini me), is that he also 'suffers' from mild dyslexia, but luckily his condition was spotted a lot sooner than mine. That culminated in me being able to provide the best education for him and he went from a mainstream school into private schooling where he could get more one-on-one time. The extra tuition with his Maths and English in particular led him from being quite poor academically into being top of the class.

Private education worked so well for Carwyn that the decision was made between my ex-wife and myself for Emyr and Llinos to also go through private schooling. I know it's very expensive but it's a very sound investment and I'm so proud of my achievements for our children.

I have always been into cars and motorbikes, basically anything with tyres on it! I used to get old Ford Escort cars, take an engine out of a 3 Litre/2.8i Capri or Ford Granada, then cut and weld the body of a Ford Escort car to make this bigger engine fit, then upgrade the whole car. I used to go rally driving in amateur rallies and it was a bit of fun, I didn't have a lot of money but I managed to do all the mechanics myself as a youngster and enjoyed that immensely. One car I'd always, always dreamt of was an Aston Martin, and when the Aston Martin DB9 came out, I thought I'd love to own one of them and drive it.

It was on my wish list, it was one of my goals for rewarding myself once I had enough spare cash. This materialised five years after starting investing, I went to the dealership and I thought, I'm not buying a brand new Aston Martin, because like most cars and equipment when you buy something new, immediately it comes out the showroom it drops by around a third in value.

I thought if I buy a second-hand one that's nearly new, then this will be a far better deal, and I knew the particular specification of car I wanted, it was going to be a blue one and in fact the colour was called Celeste Blue. I wanted blue leather in it called

Blue Haze leather. I know I was narrowing my options down, however, I wanted to hunt around for a car that had very low mileage, had been well looked after, and like new.

I went to Stratstone dealers in Cardiff and I noted the price in my mind that I wanted to pay. I went there with a T-shirt and jeans on, in my beat up old Citroen. I turned up and I could see the look of disdain from the car salesmen in their very well pressed shirts and smart suits. I think they thought I was a time waster. I'd never driven an Aston Martin DB9 so the first thing I wanted to do was arrange to test drive one. That was a heck of a job when they thought I wasn't serious, but I managed to book a test drive, not for that day, but to come back a few days later and take their demo out, after signing all of these forms which protected them in case I crashed the car!

I used to rally drive so I could handle a car fairly well and on the test drive we went up to a big car park complex in Newport and I really 'put it to go'. Sitting next to me in the passenger seat was the salesman, he was shouting at the top of his voice "Slow down! Stop you idiot!" Obviously I ignored him because the noise of the car was so great! It was superb fun to see what the car could really do as it was so balanced to drive. Astons DB9's are 50-50 weight distribution over the axles. I had it sliding in a spin in this big car park and I could control it exactly to where I wanted it to go and I thought 'that's it, I'm definitely getting one of these'.

So after being told off by the salesman for being reckless and immature, we got back to the showroom and I stated to him exactly what car specification I was looking for. He then required proof of funds which I quickly had sent through. Immediately there was a complete change in the guy from looking at me as if I was time waster to "Oh Mr. Green would you like to join us for a coffee, do sit down" and all of the 'rubbish stuff' that comes with buying a prestigious product. He asked, "Would you like to visit the Aston Martin factory?" What a total turnaround and within two days they had found the car within the dealership network which matched my criteria, but they wanted £12,000 more than I was willing to pay.

The negotiations began and I managed to get the price down to very close to the maximum I would pay, by saying to them, "If I don't buy through the dealership, I've found cars cheaper elsewhere in

Exchange and Mart and Private Sale, so I'll go that route." They were warning me against that because it wouldn't be dealer checked etc. Actually I'd rather buy through the dealer and just knew it was a good negotiating tool at the time.

I wanted to help my credit rating and credit score, and even though I had surplus spare funds to pay in cash, I put the whole amount on my credit card. I remember as they swiped the credit card this look towards me of "I don't think this payment's going to go through," as it was rather a large amount. But I had already pre-authorised my credit card to the company; they knew it was coming and the payment flew through.

They fussed around me so much because the payment had now been made, and I was smiling to myself as I drove the car away and thinking I'm really now starting to live that dream and to this day I still have the same Aston Martin and it's an absolute beauty.

I have done two slight modifications on it, a Larini stainless steel exhaust system because it has a lovely reverberation in the noise and it's had a little bit of engine mapping, just to create a bit more efficiency, I love it and it's lots of fun.

I'm not; however, too flash with luxury things, that's why I still have the same car. It's nice to drive something that you've really wanted and it is good reward for your hard work and effort .One of my beliefs I live by is,

Never borrow to buy a luxury

My kids love swimming and they have all passed their Lifesavers, we have always loved the water. They said "Dad, will you buy us a Jet Ski so we can all go out together?" My sons knew that you could get big jet skis that you can actually water-ski behind. I heard that an associate in Spain who had gone through hard times was selling off a lot of equipment, he had a lot of 'toys' in his garage, amongst them there was this big jet ski. I made him a cheeky offer, and I bought it. I'm so careful with my money I didn't even have it shipped back to the UK, it was a good excuse for me to go and pick it up and tow it back to Wales after stopping over in Spain for a couple of days break. We've had hours and hours of fun, on the sea, near where we live. It's important to have an activity that the whole family enjoys. To hear the laughter and joyous screams of my children and their friends when they are messing around on the water, that's what life's all about.

Left to right, Me, Carwyn, Llinos, Emyr enjoying 'Hobie Cat' sailing.

$\mathcal{R}$ich $\mathcal{R}$ule 5

You are only as good as the people you surround yourself with

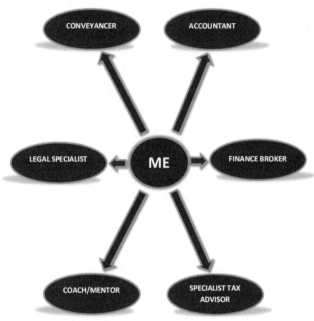

- Accountant
- Finance broker
- Specialist tax adviser
- Legal Specialist
- Conveyancer
- Coach/Mentor

The Accountant needs to be used to your business sector. The accounts can largely be done by yourself or your finance manager and then passed on to the accountant for scrutiny. The accountant is more a book keeper than an advisor, however whatever systems you use in your office they need to be compatible with your firm of accountants. We use QuickBooks™ in our office, but equally you can use Sage™ or any other accountancy package. As long as it is compatible because then it cuts down the cost to you as a business person as it's easy to relay all the information across to the bookkeeper or accountant.

The Finance Broker needs to be 'all of the market' which means they are not tied to specific lenders but have access to all products on the market place. The broker ideally should also be well qualified, either chartered or a fellow ensuring better financial support. Unfortunately there are still a number of lesser qualified brokers in the market place who will find you the mortgage or loan that pays them the most commission rather than finding you the most cost effective options.

The Specialist Tax Advisor is different from your accountant, they are going to charge a higher rate per hour and we wouldn't want that person necessarily scrutinising our book keeping because it would be too costly to take that approach, which is why you need the two separate people. The tax advisor and accountant obviously need to liaise with each other and with ourselves, and regular meetings on planning the way forward are extremely important here – I will come back to that point in a few moments.

The Legal Specialist is on board for any legal litigation, recovery of debt of monies owed, or for most other legal services that may be required for the type of business that you are operating. Again finding and engaging with these people before you require their services is important because often times you have to move fast on the legal angle of something when it arises.

The Conveyancer who's dealing with our property purchases and transactions again is a very important member on our team. They need to work efficiently to carry out all the property searches quickly on your behalf when purchasing or selling, and need to be cost effective at the same time.

The Coach/Mentor, most people who are very successful in business have at least one business coach or mentor that they turn to in order to bounce ideas off or to gain advice and empowerment to push forwards and grow themselves both personally and in a business capacity. That is certainly the case with myself, although my story is slightly more quirky than some where one of my mentors who inspires me is Sandie.

I met Sandie when I went to look at a smallholding she owns with a view to buying it and developing the barns for resale and profit. On arrival at the property I could see her smallholding was ideal for this option, however, there was something about Sandie that led me to help her with her finances so she could stay at the property. This basically consisted of restructuring her mortgage to a new provider at a cheaper rate of interest. As mentioned previously Sandie is a healer, however, she also carries out Soul Clearing, but I did not know any of this when I first met her on this viewing. As a result of me helping her out she told me a little about what she did and I was totally intrigued. On investigating further I found out that Soul Clearing removes the energy blocks that one may have which can block success or other important areas within your life. A Soul Clearer will generally use their spirit guides to engage with your spirit guides. The guides send messages across between each other then back to Sandie who acts as a portal to sort out your energy blocks, seems strange eh?!

When I first discovered this, I felt it was a little bit off the wall! Sandie had highlighted there were two blocks in my life that I possibly needed help with.

The two energy blocks in my life at that time were struggling with feelings of underachievement and also that I could not see a clear way forward with the divorce settlement. Both of these energy blocks were removed from me by Sandie and from that point forward the achievements rocketed and the divorce settlement, especially concerning the children's 50/50 custody, was quickly concluded between Lynwen and myself.

She said that as long as I intended to be clear then that intention was powerful enough for her to get her guides to work with my guides and clear any energy problems.
I remember the day that I said, "Yes I am up for that, I will agree to the Soul Clearing."

She asked me a few questions over the telephone and then said "Phone me back in the morning and tell me how you feel."

I went to bed that evening intending strongly to be clear of any energy blocks but still not quite sure of what the outcome was going to be. When I woke up in the morning it was quite wonderful because I could actually hear the birds singing and I had not really noticed that before and I could really smell the aromas, the whole world seemed a brighter and a happier place! I phoned Sandie back and relayed this information across and her response was "There you are, you are clear now, intend to remain clear and grounded, that means keep your feet on the ground, and you will be fine".

On my life's journey, I remembered certain comments, particularly from people I interviewed during the Nuffield scholarship, comments such as "Don't let anybody break your spirit" and "Keep your spirits high" and I wondered whether this was related in any way to this experience that I had just encountered with Sandie the Soul Clearer. I believe it was. Soul Clearing is sometimes spoken of amongst leading entrepreneurs but mostly remains unsaid or is denied.

We have looked at the basic considerations for business structures and management, I'd like to move on now to how we put this in place.

I will share some advice that Sir Richard Branson gave me. He said in business one of the most important points is to:

Become the observer in business.

In Wales for instance it could refer to the benefit of not being the coalminer at the face of the mine mining the coal, but being the owner of the mine who is overseeing all operations. Richard explained it to me in the way that it's almost like going up in a helicopter and looking down on your life and businesses and thinking objectively on your outcomes from that vantage point.
Step back from the day-to-day hassle and bustle, chill out, and oversee from that position. I have found this to be extremely advantageous, especially when situations arise during a particularly busy period and things need sorting out immediately. This approach helps one to keep a clear mind, remain grounded, and think objectively on outcomes.

We can have the best businesses in the world but if we have the wrong team it can all come crashing down. I regularly focus on my team. I've become **Head of Happiness;** I make sure that all team members are happy in their positions and happy with the way forward on their **Wealth and Happiness** journey.

Some of the fastest-growing businesses adopt a similar approach in the way they run their operations. I remember speaking with Richard Reed of Innocent Smoothies. He explained to me that the bright colours, quirky furnishings, relaxed dress style and approach that he adopted in his business encouraged creativity amongst his team. Getting feedback from your team is vital. Some of the feedback and ideas from our team are absolutely brilliant. Happy people create better solutions for business growth.

We manage **Happiness** within our team by holding monthly **Performance Review** meetings at our office, where all team members can raise any points they wish in any area of our businesses. I share an overview of our past performance and immediate short-term and longer term goals.

Another personal management action that is proving fruitful across our business is monitoring monies at the bank together with Profit and Loss accounts on a weekly basis.

Every Friday my Finance Manager will e-mail me that information which is also trended on a spreadsheet. This is great for monitoring the bottom line returns of business.
I first look at the trend of money at the bank in each business, has it gone up or down? Then compare the changes with the previous week. Once I have looked at the monies at the bank I will look at the Profit and Loss spreadsheets to determine why there are differences.

It has contributed to success in my structures as at a glance we can see areas where profits are flourishing and areas where they are not doing particularly well. We can make a decision as to whether we continue with that particular product or service, or actually cut our losses early and move on.

It's quite interesting with the property portfolio because a large percentage of the property we rent out is to tenants who claim income support from the Government. The problem for us is the UK Government pays out this money either weekly or four weekly. With there being more than four weeks in a month this can throw off the income figures slightly on that business, whereby one particular week there can be quite a large surplus of money at the bank and then another week it can reduce dramatically because we're waiting for payments to be made into the account.

This is where the trending is important, **the trend is my friend**. When it comes to reviewing the money at the bank, and profit and loss accounts, it's very easy for me to cast my eyes over them to make a management decision based on the figures and facts in front of me. The whole process of overview of this information takes fifteen to twenty minutes once a week, wherever I am in the world.

Business structures and management change is an ongoing process, you should not start a business if you are not prepared to input. I made a mistake on the dairy farm in the second year when we had a manager in place of actually delegating too much responsibility. It went from the first year where I interfered too much with the decisions the manager was making, into the second year with a different manager where I stepped back far too much.

I've learnt there is a happy medium of engagement with your key personnel and your team where monitoring can take place without overdue interference.

Delegate but don't abdicate your leadership responsibilities.

$\mathcal{R}$ich $\mathcal{R}$ule 6

Know your business weaknesses

Mistakes most people make when starting a business:

The most important factor is to have the right attitude towards your business. Many people have an attitude which is not conducive to success. For instance many feel that they possibly won't succeed. Remember if you think you are going to fail, or you think you can win, then you will. It comes back to the power of the law of attraction. Also, having an overpowering ego can hinder your development success.

When people keep talking about how good they are it really does annoy others, and humility is a wonderful attribute that needs to be learnt by some.

People like doing business with people they like, and people generally like people who are like themselves, so a good business person would be quite humble, possess good integrity, and

$\mathcal{R}$ich
$\mathcal{R}$ules
Steps to
Wealth &
Happiness

always look to serve their customers extremely well. Any attitude that doesn't contain those qualities could be detrimental to their business growth.

I've noticed a lot of people who just chase the money and that's not conducive to long-term successful business. Those types of people can sometimes make multi-millions but they generally tend to lose it just as quickly.

It's one thing making money; it's another thing keeping it

When starting a business, start from a position of strength, whereby you have integrity, you look after your customers first and serve their needs. Remember that whatever product or service you engage in, the customer is always right.

If you are getting into a very strong position financially don't brag about it. People who gain true **Wealth** often don't talk too openly about it. It's more likely to be the 'wannabe millionaires' who tend to be the ones who are extremely vocal about how much money they are allegedly making when quite often the reality is they are struggling and living beyond their financial means.

Attitude will determine your altitude in business

Concentrate on your supply side when it comes to materials or service. I get annoyed when a product is not delivered on time, or when promised. I probably would never use that service or product supplier again. Good business practice is centered around you finding the right people who can provide the right source materials or service to your business as agreed, and that isn't always the easiest. Good business people don't suffer fools gladly.

People often make mistakes in business when they lack the knowledge in that sector. You must learn your business extremely well and be the best that you can be in that sector.

I would not invest in a business that I didn't understand. I'd need to know the inside outs of that business first, so that I'd know my investment, or that of my investors who I am investing on behalf of, are as safe as possible.

Always invest in some good quality training, it pays

dividends. However be careful, in the marketplace a number of training providers do not act on the advice they give others!

People who make mistakes often don't stipulate clear goals and boundaries, this is extremely important. A typical entrepreneur can change their mind quite quickly, and I can bear witness to the fact that my natural state is to want to try everything and run the risk of finishing nothing. I have to align myself to my goals and stick with them. I write my goals down and I write the action plan to achieving those goals.

The goals need to be clear, they need to be realistic, achievable, and come from your heart not your head. There is no point setting goals that you don't enjoy. If you don't enjoy it you're more likely to fail.

Manage your expectations, many people approach me and say "I want to be a millionaire by this time next year." It's possible but unlikely, it takes time and it takes hard work and if you've got expectations which are far too high, you can get disheartened.

Manage expectations from other people; remember we are all only human at the end of the day.

I see huge mistakes being made where business owners do not control their business. As a result many people are fearful of setting up their own business and prefer the 'safety net' of a franchise or a 'white label' (rights to sell a product/s or service) or going into partnership with another. A franchise or white label product or the wrong partners are ingredients for a higher chance of failure in my opinion. I'm not a big fan of buying into franchises or white labelling because the only person getting truly wealthy in a franchise is usually the person who owns it. I'd rather own the business myself and be controlling that business. In fact I don't run any franchises whatsoever because I don't truly believe in them.

I tried multi-level marketing once and it relied on my people down line selling products so that I would get commission. It was damn hard work for me to empower those people to sell and I found that I had no ownership of that business. I was making some cash flow and because I didn't own the business I could not capitalise on the worth of that business, unlike property and other business ownerships.

Generally in a company or business the more we increase the profits, the more that business is worth.

Some years ago, I made the mistake of partnering up with a person on a land deal. My gut feel initially was that he was a little bit greedy, however, giving him the benefit of the doubt, I went ahead with the deal. I should have listened to my gut feel, but I used to be too much of a giver and give people the benefit of the doubt. The partnership turned ugly and it cost me a lot of monies to legally dissolve it. Lesson learnt. Always listen to your intuition!

I would never get into any form of joint-venture or partnership without a clear partnership agreement, highlighting the roles and responsibilities of each of the partners, and should it turn to custard, what the exit strategies are. Now I check the people out thoroughly and I listen to my intuition.

Don't over capitalise your business start-up. Many borrow far too much money on a business structure that doesn't make profits in the medium term. They often blame everything else but themselves at the end of the day.

The Rich Rules
Steps to
Wealth &
Happiness

If your borrowings are too high against your income, i.e. you've over capitalised your business start-up, then you're fighting a losing battle in a lot of cases. I prefer starting small with business like the peanut principle I mentioned in Rich Rule 3. It's not the first million that has to be made straight away, it's the first hundred pounds and then the thousand pounds and then the five thousand pounds profit. Start building up generic business growth, you can argue it can take slightly longer that way but at least you are taking a safe and sure approach when you adopt the **peanut principle** to business as opposed to the 'boom and bust' type scenario which some people employ.

I often refer to the three S's when I'm looking at hedging against mistakes in business start-up.

The three *S*'s are as follows:

1. *S***afety**

2. *(S)***Certainty**

3. *S***peed**

I know people laugh when I mention that one, because 'certainty' starts with a 'C', that's me being mildly dyslexic.

I've learned in business that:

Opportunities are never lost, it's just that somebody else will take the ones you miss

If you've done your research and networking properly, it passes all the financial criteria, and it fits with what you love to do, then do it!

We can never be 100% sure about anything in life, we must jump on board and do it, because at the end of the day that's the only way that you're going to make your business successful.

I remember reading a book before I started growing multiple business structures that was written by Stephen R Covey called The Seven Habits of Highly Effective People. I related to the seven habits that Stephen referred to and in particular I really liked Stephen's approach to our time at death. I know it's perhaps a little bit morbid but Stephen had two examples which he asked readers to consider.

1. What do you want written on your
   gravestone? This would say a lot about you in
   your life.

I thought long and hard about what I wanted on my
gravestone. Initially I wrote "Here lies Kevin Green,
he helped people and left the world a better place."
Then over time I thought, no, that's a bit too
mushy, that's what everybody would put on their
gravestone, let's do something a little bit more
succinct.

This is what I will have on my gravestone:

2   You are in your rocking chair at the end of
    your life, what will you be saying?

I'll tell you what he suggested and I agree with this,
that most people would be rocking their rocking
chair really slowly. They'll be looking back on a life
with a lot of regret, saying things like 'I wish I'd
done more with my life." That's a bad position to
be in because regret can eat away at you.
I know I'll be sat there in the rocking chair, in a
good few years' time from now! I will be rocking
that rocking chair flat out, with smoke coming off
the rockers. I'll have my right hand and my thumb
up saying "Spot on, I've given it a go and I've
enjoyed it."

Now part of my enjoyment comes from
empowering others, the ability to give back to
society is a wonderful gift. I engage with a lot of
people who really want to give big time, but the
mistake they make is they are too charitable too
early on. They are trying to start their business and
also they're giving large amounts of their time and
money to their favourite charity.

I'm very mindful of the saying that charity begins at
home, and I'm also mindful that if we look after

number one, that's yourself, and get yourself in a very strong position both financially and time wise, then you can give back so much more to charity. I'm a social entrepreneur, which means we like to give back. I give back on a constructive basis and I have got strong links to three of my favourite charities, and the top one is Make-A-Wish Foundation UK.

Having lost my sister at a young age, I am very aware that there are young people and their families who need help. I love being involved, helping bring joy to those young people who may be far less fortunate than myself. Helping to grant a magical wish is priceless.

People don't test the product or service in the market and this is vital. Look at what your competitors do, and see if you can do it better. Perhaps use survey programs and social media sites to test your ideas, because at the end of the day if you go blind in a marketplace and you go forward with what you think or feel is the best product or service, that may not turn out to be the case. I've seen many people fail in this area, where they have a passion for something, they set up a business around it, yet they did not ask the masses whether that's a product or service that they would want.

Does your product or service have long term appeal? When we look at something like mobile phone applications, at the moment they are hugely popular, but the IT world moves very, very fast and my prediction would be that they will be overtaken by the new best thing in no time. So if you've got a business supplying mobile phone apps to help companies make money and you sell the business in 20 years' time perhaps that could be too far down the line.

The timing of sale of any business is important. Huge mistakes are made when that product or service loses appeal and then the business person tries to off load it. The best time to sell a business is generally after it's been in operation for at least two years, but is still gaining popularity with the public. It has that public appeal, and a strong net profit spreadsheet is important. At the end of the day, don't leave it too late before selling your business, sometimes we hold onto our 'baby' too long, so timing of sale is absolutely vital in some cases.

Rich Rule 7

Know how to raise capital

Funding consolidation and capitalisation of business

Consider the timing to clear debt when you're growing a business. If you don't pay down some debt, you will find it very difficult to get further lending from the banks and other lending institutions going forward.

Stages to consolidating, lowering gearing and making the business a lot safer before further business growth are paramount. Once we start clearing down debt we can then go back to lenders if need be and borrow again to grow our business or borrow for a new business start-up.

With a debt to equity ratio no greater than 50% we can then possibly look at further leveraging.

If all signs are that the business is turning sour and its profits are on the way down, then do think about cutting those losses and capitalising on that business early.

Far better to get out early from a 'sinking ship' where business is concerned than to go down with it.

I often picture business as a big ship sailing towards a port, which would be the goal that you are heading for. But on that ship you have got some lifeboats and these would be our exit strategies. We should continually think about what those exit strategies would be. What the alternatives would be. Do we actually have to change our goals? Change the direction of the ship altogether? If not, then do we have to bail out and get into those lifeboats?

That's really sensible business planning, knowing that not all businesses fly, and that they could be a failure. In fact most entrepreneurs I know have failed at something somewhere along the line and I'm no different. Although I've not lost any significant money in a business, not every strategy has absolutely flown, and sometimes we need to exit early.

Focus on the bigger picture, the structure that you hold your business in as you grow the business.

You need to start thinking about whether you go into a company, if it's not already in one.
It's generally easy enough to transfer the business into a company, but you will need some very sound tax advice if you are going for that new move, because although it's easy enough to transfer a business into a company at any time along its timeline, it is very difficult to disband it back from the company structure without some significant tax liabilities.

I'm not a big fan of tax shielding structures and all the grey areas with tax, it's probably inviting problems into your business if you are going to go down that route, and I have certainly hedged against that and stuck to a clear system as far as ownership structures are concerned. What I do like are trust structures, to transfer assets into a trust can have many benefits when you are looking at consolidating business and making it safer perhaps to transfer onto our dependents.

In my case, the main focus is my three children and it's no good me making the money and taking all the **Wealth** to the deathbed and leaving them with a massive Inheritance Tax liability. I have to think sensibly while I'm consolidating and growing business of how I'm going to best use those assets for the benefit of my children.

What I've put in place as a structure for each of my children is a form of trust which is called a beneficiary trust. This works particularly well for my needs and something perhaps you may consider if you are looking at leaving your assets to another before death.

With land and property there are some fantastic gift away rules in the UK where you can gift away and live for seven years after the deed of gift, and this can nullify in a lot of cases the Inheritance Tax liability on the estate. When it comes to property it's certainly an interesting option a lot of investors opt for.

An interesting story came to light on this regarding the Queen Mother who had not planned for Inheritance Tax before she died. When she got to ninety two and a half years of age, she allegedly said to her tax adviser something along the lines of "One would like to save tax, especially Inheritance Tax. What should one do?" The advice to her in layman's terms was "Well Ma'am, you are a bit limited, you have left it a little bit late, the only rule left to you is the seven year gift away rule," and the tax adviser at that time explained to the Queen Mother that if she gifted away and only lived half of the seven years then the tax liability to her beneficiaries would be half because the length of time was seven years. It works like a taper and the longer she lived through that term, the less tax they would have to pay. If she lived the whole of the seven years after the deed of gift there would be no tax to pay on the Crown estate. It's said that the Queen Mother liked this idea and she said in layman's terms "That's spot on, I'll have some of that, let's go for that tax break."

She then gifted away assets, now interestingly she didn't gift big assets to the Queen and Prince Philip, it's alleged she actually gifted much further down the family line, to William and Harry. That was a wise move perhaps on her part because we don't know whether this gift away rule for Inheritance Tax will remain, but whilst it's in our lifetime it's a good one to consider.

Now it is said, and I reference the press and media here, the Queen Mother, once she had gifted away, did live for seven years and two and a half weeks before she passed away, totally avoiding any Inheritance Tax liability on the Crown estate.

That on her part was an extremely wise move, and I often wondered to myself, did she live those extra years and months and 'will' herself on, just to save those millions that would have been incurred on the Inheritance Tax liability!

Going back to my own situation on trust structures and beneficiary trusts, I've done something which is quite quirky and interesting and I believe encourages entrepreneurship in my three children.

I asked my tax adviser if I could put in place a beneficiary trust with a form of match release fund whereby my children would have to show the trustees of the beneficiary trust that they made £1000 before they could release £1000 from the trust. The advice I had at that time was yes that could be done.

So it was duly drawn up whereby my children received certain release of benefit from the beneficiary trust on their birth dates. I realised that my children would need monies at eighteen, twenty one and twenty five, should they go to university and mostly it would be handy if they needed to release some monies.

But remember they'd have to show the trustees they'd made the money before they could match fund and release the same amount.

This was all set up and I was quite happy about the structure as it was satisfying my big in-depth **Happiness** for transferring **Wealth** to my children.

I shared with my children the simple story of what I had done, setting up the trust and why I had done it. I then shared with them about the match release fund that they would have to raise one thousand pounds and show it to the trustees to release a further one thousand from the trust.

Carwyn raised a question, "So Dad, if I earn a thousand pounds from a business or from a job, I can take that to the trustees and I have the possibility of releasing a further thousand pounds?"
I said, "That's right son, that's spot on."
He said, "So Dad how much have I got now?"
"You have two thousand pounds son." I replied.
He said, "So I can now take this two thousand pounds back to the trustees and match release a further two thousand pounds?"
Actually he was right, he was going to use the

trust money to further leverage money from the trust itself. I thought, "Uh oh, I've made a mistake." So it was a great moment for me to think my kids are actually smarter than I am. I had to go back to my legal specialist and asked her to put an addendum into the trust documentation to make sure that it was new money that the kids had to earn, not trust release money. I duly told Llinos and Emyr that this was the case and they thought it was quite hilarious as well, that Carwyn had found this loophole in what I had put together, a straightforward loophole too which I'd missed.

Lovely moments when you realise your kids are smarter than you!

Going forward think about how you can pass on potential **Wealth** that you have accumulated, because to set tax planning aside and not think about it at the beginning could be naïve. Before we start business growth and business consolidation even at business start-up, we need to be thinking what our outcomes are for the whole of the business. One thing is for sure you are going to die, hopefully not for some years, but it is something that needs to be considered. Think about how that transfer of those assets is going to take place and should it be implemented way before that time.

Certainly this is where having good people around us is so important. A really good tax adviser who understands your business is well worth the money every time. I think you've heard the expression 'if you pay peanuts, you get monkeys' and this is certainly the case, and in my experience there are a lot of people who offer a cheap deal and on occasions have not delivered the best service.

As far as this goes you really need to aim high and get the best advice that you can, because in the long term it will save you a huge amount of pain and suffering down the line.

Going back to my structure with property and the consolidation of that business as far capital is concerned, remember, I have a very clear rule on debt clearance, the **three-two-one rule.**

I also endeavor to totally clear debt on the properties I hold as rentals by year 10.

Once the debt has been cleared on a house look at the consideration of placing that house into a trust fund, a very simple planning process within the portfolio.

The other businesses and companies usually have a timeline before I sell them. There are a few that I will keep right through to the inheritance tax transfer stage with the exception of rental property.

I feel that's good business planning, to trade businesses, 'a bird in the hand is worth two in the bush'. We often notice that when we sell a business, we have a good 'payday' for that. We can then build a platform from there going forward and starting another new business and/or begin clearing down debt in other existing business structures. I always view debt as a bridging facility only; I'm never a person who likes debt on a very long-term basis.

I know others may differ on their views on this, and if I wanted to be a multibillionaire and risk a little bit more then maybe I'd leverage more, but I don't want to be that way, I like investing safely, and I've got what I need for my family.

When it comes to fast business growth, and as I have mentioned previously, one of the best ways

I've achieved that is profit-sharing with the manager or people involved with the businesses. I'm not a huge fan of giving away ownership or shareholding although I am a fan of sharing the success of the business by splitting the cash flow profit. That's quite a simple approach and it's mutually beneficial.

Companies and businesses are valued mainly on two main criteria:

1. <u>Firstly</u> is track record, how long they've been in business and how well they've done.
2. <u>Second</u> is future 'pipeline' of orders for that product or service.

 Those two main points will be coupled with financial criteria, obviously the more profit a business can make, the more value that business will achieve if it were to be sold.

I remember my youngest son years ago, before I'd started on this quest in major businesses, telling me, "Dad, you've got potential." I remember that very clearly because at that time that's all I did have, potential, and I did not want written on my gravestone, "Here lies Kevin Green, died with his potential intact." That was going to be a big

The
Rich
Rules

Steps to
Wealth &
Happiness

no-no as far as I was concerned, and I feel I've achieved a certain amount of my potential to date, and my children have recognised that and they've been empowered by it.

Funding Options

There are a number of ways that we can access monies. The modern world is becoming more diverse, and interestingly enough it's said that banks are not now the obvious route for obtaining money for business start-ups or business development. In fact a lot of the general public don't trust the banks perhaps as much as they would have done in the past because of all the libel scams, misuse of funds, bad advice etc that's been in the press recently. The banks are having a bit of a rough time, and rightly or wrongly people are looking elsewhere for other funding options. I would not discount the banks altogether, the banks play at a very major role in what we do and they've been very helpful to me. The relationships I've had, and still do have, with certain bank managers, have been very important to me, and they've backed me when others would not, because I've always delivered what I said I would with regards to the return of finances on many business propositions.

It does pay though to shop around, we are on the world market and there are a number of major clearing banks who may well support you.

However, the alternatives to the banks are becoming more and more interesting. The private funding market is starting to boom right across the world and I've been very interested in this right from the conception stage. In 2008 I started looking a lot deeper into how I could 'become a bank' so to speak, although we can't actually use that term 'become a bank', we become 'like a bank', in that we can access money and then use that for property and business deals, and it led to me investigating in-depth the whole structure of the way that banks work. Basically it works as follows, people save money on deposit with a current account or a high interest return account in a bank, they get paid an interest rate which arguably is not huge, and the banks then have millions on deposit from customers.

The interesting bit is what happens to that money. The banks make money on the customer's money, because on the other side the simplest thing they do with it is lend it back out to people who want to borrow money, but they lend it out at a much higher interest rate than they pay the savers who have deposited that same money with them. The margin can be quite a wide margin, but in a lot of cases the bank has some risk involved.

I wondered though was it possible to cut out the middleman, cut out the bank, and go straight to the private saver and offer them a higher return on their money.

As I was mulling this over the term 'crowd funding' started coming into the marketplace. I was interested first of all in how these online platforms would be operating; they were just starting off then in the conceptual basis, but soon in the months to follow they became a reality, whereby a borrower could look for a lender or a number of lenders to lend onto his or her investment proposal.

As this idea developed and companies started springing up offering crowd funding opportunities, the term 'peer to peer' lending entered the marketplace. This was of particular interest to me because I felt this could be the solution to a lot of private funding options, where one peer or a few peers lend to another i.e. the people who want a higher return on their savings would look at a borrower's proposal and put their money into that.

Now my view on this is that it can be higher risk for the saver who wants a higher return if they're not careful.

However, I actively sought advice from the Office of Fair Trading and looked at how we could set up our own business as a peer-to-peer type operation. I was told which licenses I would require, so we set up a company and we applied for the licenses and after quite a bit of work we were granted the licensing. Now this culminated with a big change in the whole of the financial sector from the Financial Services Authority changing to the Financial Conduct Authority, and the Financial Conduct Authority (FCA) taking over all the operations of the Office of Fair Trading, so that any licenses or any aspect of the governance of financial institutions and structures would come under the remit of the FCA. We were informed of these changes by the FCA and were told we needed to reapply for interim permissions for certain licenses, which were consumer credit based licenses, in order to update our operation.

So we duly took legal advice on this from a leading firm of solicitors in the UK and we then applied for the licenses. We adopted the approach with peer-to-peer that it would be far safer for lenders if lending was not done through an online platform, but went back to old-fashioned banking where a saver could meet with us face-to-face and we could match them up with a borrower, who again would have a face-to-face meet. The borrower's proposal would only be allowed to go forward once our loan assessment team had looked in depth at their proposal and made sure on a risk category that it wasn't a high risk investment proposal.

Also we planned to ask for security from the borrower for the lenders benefit. So it was far safer for the lender to invest the money in the borrower's proposal. As it turned out, this is the structure that's been most favoured by the Financial Conduct Authority.

Unfortunately the UK has payday lenders who are charging extortionate interest rates and annual percentage rates of interest to customers for short-term lending of money. The term 'payday lender' derives from institutions that would lend money to a person until payday.
The payday lenders often prey on the individuals who are in the most financial difficulty. I believe there are companies who are charging up to

4000% APR. It is unfair, it's just wrong; it should be about treating customers fairly.

Moving forward it is highly likely that the draft policy with the FCA today is going to change. The FCA in their policy guidelines favour lower APR. They may well make this law, which will outlaw these payday lenders and more fall into line with favouring peer-to-peer type operations. Obviously the offer of security by the borrower makes the investment proposal sound and safe. I particularly like the peer-to-peer structure; I believe it is going to get some bad press however, because there are some questionable operators in any field.

If the borrower is offering security, the interest rates on the money are kept sensible, and the peer-to-peer arranger or broker is not taking a massive cut for themselves, then I feel the business will continue and grow into being one of the major lending options in the whole world. This seems to be the case so it will be interesting to observe developments in lending.

The next area of interest for raising money is grants and incentives from Government. Often business people don't investigate what support there is available from the UK Government and from Governments worldwide.

Usually the focus for Government money is whether a business creates jobs. The Government is more likely to offer grants and incentives to that structure than any other.

So business planning is important, especially in the medium and longer term planning to show the Government exactly what the proposal is as far as job creation and growth. I'm quite fortunate to have been asked recently to sit on the Welsh Governance advisory panel for entrepreneurship as one of five team members who directly advise the minister. It is quite an eye-opener being involved in Government policy and seeing why decisions are made in certain ways. I fully understand and support the job creation side of the equation and it makes sense that rather than support individuals who are self-employed and don't intend to grow their structures it would make more sense to support businesses that intend to employ.

These Government loans and grants range from helping with IT equipment in the office, right up to business start-up and business growth in a number of categories that vary widely. It takes a bit of digging on your part as a business person to see what grants are available in your country and in your area but certainly well worth the time researching out exactly what you can get. Very often with grant basis there are stipulations e.g. if you were to draw down a grant and then sell the business within a short term then you may have to pay all or part of that grant back.

In the past I've been fortunate enough to draw down some renovation grants for property, also some IT support money for growth in our office. A stipulation on both of those grants were that we had to be in business for a minimum term of five years post the date of the grant drawdown. Again this makes perfect sense as far as we were concerned, because we intended to be in the game for the longer term.

When it comes to funding options the diamonds are quite often under our feet, in that family members or associates can have big monies deposited on account actually earning very little interest return. It makes sense perhaps for us to offer them a higher return on their money and then gain access to that funding for investment purposes.

I personally would prefer if the investor is offered security in some form, it's easy enough to put a charge on an asset for their benefit rather than look at unsecured lending which is higher risk.

The private investment market is interesting on that front, however be sure that if it's friends and family that you're dealing with, follow the normal legal procedures on a funding option and set up a safe loan agreement signed by both parties and witnessed by a notable independent. Quite often relationships can turn to custard and sometimes these little niggles become big arguments. It's also safer for all parties concerned if a partnership agreement is put in place with clear outlines as to the roles and responsibilities of each of the parties in the agreement documentation.

Angel funding, private investors as well as joint-venture partners are all a possibility. Obviously I have made it quite clear that I don't particularly like giving away ownership of a business unless I really have to, but if you do decide to go down that route, try wherever possible to maintain the major shareholding or the major ownership of the business or company so that you have the major control. I know a lot of businesses will look at going public and that's a major decision. It's a great way to raise funds but here we are really looking at what we do before that point, how do we maximise what we've got before we decide to create a major PLC. Going public with a company is something I personally have not done, therefore I would feel limited going into depth about that at this stage, but it is something perhaps we would consider further down the line.

Finally one of the finance alternatives I've found to be extremely helpful are the use of options on payment for a service or product. Can we have time to payment day? This helped me hugely when I first started up my topsoil business which I mentioned previously, in that I could have time to pay for that product which helped my bankroll in a major way. So when those terms can be negotiated in some form of option as well, it is a consideration that needs to be kept in mind when we're looking at a proposal. One of my clear stipulations to my customers and my suppliers is if I owe monies to somebody, I want to pay it on time every time to keep my good business name, so on the flipside my financial integrity together with my personal integrity is always maintained.

$\mathcal{R}$ich $\mathcal{R}$ule 8

Know your outcomes

I truly hope that by reading this book you will achieve **Wealth and Happiness** by using the business principles I have outlined and use personally.

For me my number one priority is my family, and to be able to witness what's happening with my children is absolutely superb! All of my three children were born in February and interestingly enough my ex-wife's birthday is in May, perhaps there is a little story in there somewhere, but she is a terrific mother and between her, myself and my extended family members, my children have grown up in a safe, secure and empowering environment.

I learnt through my Nuffield scholarship study that people can become entrepreneurs. They don't have to be born or genetically wired to be an entrepreneur. If a person is placed in the right environment then as long as that person has the will, determination and passion they will absolutely blossom.

I'm very proud that my children are blossoming all in their own right. My daughter Llinos is now 21 as I write this and she's just completing her final year in university. She is studying business and media, two areas which she loves. Interestingly enough the media interest started arising on the back of a TV programme that I became involved with on Channel Four called 'Secret Millionaire.' Llinos witnessed how the programme was put together over the nine days of filming, which was condensed into a 45 minute programme. It intrigued her the way everything was done behind the scenes. Also any opportunity where I have been speaking on a major international stage she has been present. I have invited her on stage from a fairly young age and she has become a very humble yet confident presenter, commentating on TV engagements that I have been involved with. She became very excited about the whole structure, so much so, that she went on work experience two summers running with two different production companies and then she decided that was going to be part of the degree that she went for. Now I don't necessary feel that you need a degree to do well in life, there is only one PhD I've needed and it's called piling houses deep! If you have academic abilities then go for it as it's always a safety net to fall back on. Llinos is loving university, she has won a number of competitions, the most poignant one was her business idea which won awards for her idea called Yesterday's News. It's a recycling business for newspapers. When a person goes to the newsagents and buys a new newspaper they would bring their old newspaper 'Yesterday's News' with them and deposit that in the 'Yesterday's News' bin. She is very conscious of recycling and wants to support the planet. The Yesterday's News team would then visit all the newsagents on a daily basis and empty the newsagents bins, then sell that paper into recycling for profit, quite a straightforward, nicely branded and presented business. The judges of the competition liked the simplicity and the low capital start-up costs which won her and her team the top award. Some people may have argued that I had some input into that, I can tell you I didn't, it was totally her idea. Llinos has been inspired and empowered by what goes on around her and she will make a superb entrepreneur with anything she does going forward.

My son Carwyn is now 19. As I mentioned previously he struggled academically like I did at school, but with private schooling and extra concessions I'm proud to say he achieved 11 GSCEs. He then left school and chose not to go to university. He went to start a business course in the technical college but after the first day he hated it. His words to me it were, "Dad this is stuff I knew five years ago." He was only 17 at the time. I said, "Stick with it son because it's only the start. See how you go." At the end of the second day he did not want to go back to college. In his words it was a waste of his time, he was bored, and he didn't want to go back.

He had an alternative idea which was to start up an ice cream business. He needed to find an ice cream van to sell ice creams for profit.

He carried out some research and learnt that Mr. Whippy ice cream made 90% profit.

I was quite impressed by how he put his idea forward so together with his mum's approval he duly left college and further researched how to set up an ice cream business.

He found out that he needed a Level 2 Food Hygiene Certificate, a street trading license for when he pitched his ice cream van on council property, which was quite expensive in Carmarthenshire Authority coming out at ten thousand pounds a year, while also restricting him on where he could place his ice cream van.

Amongst the research he also found out he couldn't drive an ice cream van because he needed to be at least eighteen to do that, but what he could get was an ice cream bike or an ice cream trailer. So I ended up going with him to Leeds to buy a second hand ice-cream trailer that he'd found on eBay, here it is in the picture below.

Carwyn and I then attended a one day training together for the Food Hygiene Certificate. I thought I would give him some support even though I didn't really need the certificate. We took the training with a company owned by one of my coaching clients, Dawn Evans of Ajuda, Cardiff and I'm pleased to say he passed the exam with flying colours and so did I! It was a long time since I had been back at school, but it was an enjoyable day.

With the ice cream business Carwyn started making profits, he loved what he was doing and by Christmas 2013 he said, "Dad I want to buy my first house and rent it out just like you do. Would you lend me some of the money?"

I said, "I will do but you will have to save ten thousand pounds and then I will lend you the rest of the money to buy your first house." By the following February 2014 he had the ten thousand pounds. He worked very hard for it, mowing lawns, doing gardens and odd jobs. He also worked part time in our business taking property viewings and worked with the build team as an apprentice. I was very impressed with his dedication. We had some adverts running to source property and an opportunity came through for Carwyn to buy his first house.

We bought a house that needed some work and intended to fix it up and rent it out for profit. One of the proudest moments for me was when he was signing the documents for the purchase of this first house. He bought it for fifty five thousand pounds, the fix up costs were one thousand two hundred pounds, and the value now is eighty two thousand pounds.

It's rented out at five hundred and fifty pounds per month, a great return.

Carwyn (in the middle) with sellers of his 1st house.

Carwyn intends to buy a second and a third house and then sell them to create enough profit in his slush fund to cash buy the next house. He knows that it's easier to finance something you already own, so once he's got into the position that he can cash buy a property he can either trade it and sell it on for profit, or what he intends to do at that point is to follow the **three-two-one** rule and start holding onto properties which he will let out, so he will need to put a mortgage on each one to pay himself back the cash capital he has put in. **The Rich Rules** system simply works!

Carwyn signing the purchase title document of his 1st house, I am extremely proud of him.

My youngest, Emyr, loves his football and plays in the Welsh tournaments. He is 16 at present, he wants to go to university and become a sports doctor as that way he could work with the Premier League Division because he loves his football that much! Its 2015 now, Emyr is in first year Form 6 and studying business and the three main sciences Biology, Physics and Chemistry. Unlike myself, Emyr is very highly academic and finds studying at school relatively easy, which further proves that it's not always genetics that shape someone's future, it's more likely to be the environment that surrounds them, which is the biggest influence to **Wealth and Happiness.**

He trades on eBay buying and selling which he does extremely well. He is an eBay top seller and makes most of his money by finding buyers for products then linking them to people who sell those same products and taking a profit margin for himself. This method of trading is often termed as 'drop shipping' and there's very little risk as Emyr gets paid first then arranges delivery by contacting the supplier and getting them to send direct to customer.

Emyr also helps on our building projects and is showing a keen interest on all things property and business related.

Emyr is an absolute star of a young man and I'm extremely proud of all three of my children. One of the most pleasing outcomes of being a multi-millionaire is the way that it's empowered my children to achieve in life. Although it's only the beginning for them, the seeds for success have been sown and the rewards of being involved in what I've been doing is certainly paying off. I'm one very proud dad!

Am I living the dream? Yes I am. I have my fourteen pet donkeys and on February 21st 2015 one of them had a brand new baby donkey foal. As with my children most of my donkeys seem to be born in the month of February! One of those special moments in life that reminds me how lucky I am to be experiencing the great simple pleasures that nature affords us.

I have a great team of people that work with me. My team is growing and I will continue to focus on improving and expanding my businesses and look for new exciting business start-up opportunities on my journey. I love to travel the world and experience different cultures and have the opportunity to speak on major world stages alongside leading names. I feel rewarded and happy when I appear on stage and feel my hard effort over the past years was well worth it.

Turning fifty I realised I wanted to review my life goals – one of them being – motor biking. I loved motor biking as a youngster and wanted to get back on the road!

I went to the auction and purchased a repossessed motorbike which was exactly the specification of bike that I wanted. As you know by now I'm careful with my money and I would not buy a brand new bike, so just as I did with my Aston Martin I got a discounted price on a second hand machine. I follow my business principles even with lifestyle luxuries.

I bought myself a BMW R1200 GS LC. It's an absolute joy to be free spirited and jump on my bike and ride to anywhere that I please.

I'm writing this book in Spain having just jumped on the bike and driven all the way from Wales to the Costa Del Sol and loved every second of the journey.

As my story draws to a close, I'm delighted that I have been able to make a difference in so many lives. My friends are important to me, my best mate Ian is now in the property business as well as realising his dream of getting married and buying a farm for tents and touring caravans. Ian and his lovely wife, Sarah with their two young sons also have a herd of goats where they produce ice creams, smoothies and goats cheese. Ian wanted to do this from a very young age and is realising his second lifelong dream.

I became a main trainer for Robert Kiyosaki's Rich Dad Poor Dad 3 day Trainings, delivering trainings in UK for five years from February 2004 to the end of 2009. I loved my time helping Robert and Kim Kiyosaki to transform lives by delivering key wealth building strategies.

Below, myself and Robert in 2004, just after I started as a Rich Dad speaker.

My Father and Mother are full time property investors with their own expanding buy to let portfolio.

My ex-wife, Lynwen, and her new partner, are now large property investors.

Many of my close friends have started new businesses.

Sandie has become a close friend and now owns three rental properties producing great cash flow and large equity. Sandie has also set up a 'Soul Clearing' telephone business.

The feedback from people I have trained and coached is phenomenal, many have become hugely successful in achieving **Wealth and Happiness.**

I'm a very proud father of three wonderful children, all the hard effort helping with their upbringing is now paying off, and now that my kids are older there is more 'me' time.

I'm absolutely loving life which is enhanced by a successful international speaking career allowing me to travel and spread the light to others.

Rich Rule 9

Love your business(es) & 100 business ideas.

One of the most important rules to **Wealth and Happiness** is to love your business! I love what I do and I wouldn't change it for the world. If I could start again I wouldn't do anything differently. I'm happy doing exactly what I love.

I love all of my businesses. If you're passionate about what you do you will be more prepared to put in the extra effort that's often needed to make sure you gain a successful outcome.

The most important decision that any potential business person can make is choosing the right business for them. This is not a one size fits all choice. It's about choosing a business sector that you are very passionate about. Always remember to listen to your heart, your instinct, what is your gut feeling telling you about this business idea?

Does it feel right?

I also use this approach in all areas of my life.

One of the businesses I love involves coaching others, namely **Kevin Green Wealth Coach**. The initial meeting with clients is usually on a face-to-face basis; we discuss ideas and options they have available to them for a new business start-up or improving their existing business framework. I find a lot of people wish to become millionaires or multi-millionaires to achieve their own **Wealth and Happiness** but they don't know which business path to follow to live the life of their dreams. This is where a good coach or mentor can help. I particularly enjoy the experience of asking a person what their path has been from a young age, from their schooling to leaving school, and up to the point they are at today. I ask what their hobbies are and what they enjoy doing. I suggest a number of business and life options that might fit with their personality and physiology. During these discussions I look for physical changes in their demeanour as I fire different ideas at them. Often times their eyes light up, they may lean forward, unfold their arms and appear more open and engaged or smile as they hear something they love. I then know this is the idea that is most likely to bring them **Happiness**. We then discuss the commercial sense of the idea and determine whether it's also going to satisfy their **Wealth** requirements.

By default **Kevin Green Wealth Coach** training and coaching has become yet another business that I love being involved in. It could be something that perhaps you would like to set up yourself, once you too have become a very successful business person. I believe that the best coach or mentor is a person who's been there and done it.

Identifying your passions is a number one priority. I've often found people love more than one business sector and that's fine, however to love lots of different businesses and try to start them all at once may not be the best approach. Focusing fully on one or two businesses at a time and getting those absolutely flying successfully would in my view be the best approach to achieving the life of your dreams.

Drive and determination are also key in gaining success. If you have not got a very sound reason for becoming a millionaire or multi-millionaire, then don't even bother starting, because if your reason is not big enough then your business and life will probably not be very successful.

I call my main reason for achieving **Wealth and Happiness**

MY WHY?

'MY WHY' is to provide **Security and Happiness for my children.**

Work out the biggest single factor that drives you. What is your **WHY?**

Take a moment to write it down below:

MY WHY is ....
....

I'm very proud to say I've achieved **MY WHY**. I enjoy business structures so much that I will continue tweaking, starting up and growing both my own businesses and helping others realise their potential until the day I die. That coupled with the benefit of being able to truly help my favourite charities, fills me full of **Happiness.**

You will find on page 205 a list of profitable business and money saving ideas that you could consider. These are some more straightforward ideas that I've experienced, both first-hand and through third-party connections. The trick is remembering that when you set up or run a business, the mid-term goal is to step away from the front-line service. For instance if you are setting up an ironing business, you don't want to be the one actually doing the ironing in the medium-term, you would have other people helping you and perhaps profit-sharing with you to help the expansion of that business. This has been my key approach in growing multiple businesses.

100 Business Ideas

Here you will find some basic business ideas and money saving tips to help you achieve **Wealth and Happiness**:-

1) TRANSLATOR

This is a business opportunity for you if you are lucky enough to be able to speak more than one language.
A personal friend of mine and fellow Secret Millionaire, Gavin, did just that to create a very profitable translation services business. You can also outsource your work on outsourcing websites like www.odesk.com

2) LEAD GENERATOR

Being a lead generator can be a very profitable business as leads can be sold from £2 to £20 per individual industry targeted leads.

You would need to run strategic advertising campaigns to gather hot leads for specific industries that have a demand for leads, once gathered sell them on to the businesses for a profit.

3) YOGA OR SPECIFIC FITNESS INSTRUCTOR

If you are a qualified yoga, Pilates or fitness instructor run some free trial classes at a local gym to entice students and then start charging fees.

4) WEB DESIGNER

You do not have to be a professional web designer, just someone who is willing to learn and has an eye for design.
There are platforms like www.wordpress.com that make it very easy to make beautiful websites using pre designed templates. You can make more profits by upselling to shopping cart pages and ongoing

annual management packages to keep websites updated with new monthly content.

5) MAN AND VAN REMOVAL SERVICE

To start in business all you will need is a van, a mobile and a website and you are literally in business.
You will also need a waste disposal license which is obtainable from the local council, check with the environmental health officers before setting up your business. Once in business you can charge by the hour as a local removal service.

6) PROFESSIONAL BLOGGER

If you have specific knowledge about a topic that inspires you, create a niche blog and become a professional blogger. You can then sell advertising space on your blog to make good money. Blogs help websites climb up the Google classifications therefore you are also providing a search engine optimisation business at the same time.

7)   SCRAP CAR DEALER

A very worthwhile business is to remove all good condition second hand parts and sell them separately for approximately 50% of new price on sites like eBay, then send the remainder of the car shell etc to the scrap yard and weigh it in.
I personally know a South Wales based businessman who has made a fortune using this strategy.

Another idea is to contact We Buy Any Car online and buy any car in any condition, negotiate down to their lowest price possible, purchase the car and sell on for a profit.

Alternatively you can pick up scrap cars that are non-runners, have been written off or are no longer roadworthy or too costly to repair to a roadworthy condition. Buy them from £50-£500 and sell onto scrap yards for profit. New legislation has come into place in the UK which means that you cannot take home cash for scrap, the money now has to be deposited into a bank account.

8)   FISHING OR SCENIC BOAT CHARTER

If you are located by the coast, make the most of this and charge money to show people the coastline, your great fishing spots and scenic areas. Boat charter is a great way to show people fantastic fishing locations and scenic areas. Consider hire fees to charge for half day, full day or overnight fees.

9)   ACCOUNTANT

Choose what your services will be i.e.:-
Do you want to simply provide bookkeeping services for small businesses or prepare balance sheets, income statements, and other

financial reports on a monthly, quarterly, and/or annual basis?
You may consider specialising in tax accounting.

Many business owners don't mind keeping their own day-to-day bookkeeping records but would rather get professional help with their taxes.

Two of our 90 Day coaching clients, Lurie and Oxana, have set up a substantial business providing simple services to self-employed foreign workers in UK, helping them with VAT and annual accounts. They have subcontracted most of the work to self-employed individuals who speak different languages to match the needs of their clients.

10) BICYCLE REPAIR

This can be an all year round business. Rent a storage unit and offer to store people's bicycles over the winter months after you do a tune-up and any needed repairs on them. If you decide to have Saturday shop hours, you can be sure you will have a group of enthusiasts coming by to talk all things cycling. Soon you may be finding yourself selling new bikes for a major bike manufacturer.

11) BOAT CLEANING

The majority of boats are hauled out of the water for the winter or even just for mid-season repairs and will need the hull cleaned. Depending on the type of boat, it is a good time to give a major cleaning to everything else, the decks, the sleeping quarters, the head, and the holds. Start by approaching homes that have a boat sitting on the driveway. Or you could market your services to the marina on contract.

12) BUSINESS PLAN SERVICE

You could offer a comprehensive business plan service, including market research, the business plan description and the financial statements. Plan your fee around the main business that the client will want and offer the others as add-on services. You can give clients an electronic file and allow them to continue from there, or you can keep the business plan on file and offer the service of fine-tuning it whenever necessary. Have business plan samples to show clients and make sure to include your own.

13) CHIMNEY SWEEP

You could apprentice with someone who is already in the business and learn the skills that way. By becoming a chimney expert, you can combine a chimney sweep business with a chimney inspection service covering more than just whether or not the chimney needs cleaning but whether the chimney is in good working order or in need of repair. Many wood burners, Agas and Rayburns require chimney lining, perhaps another additional service you can offer to customers.

14) CLEANING SERVICE

There will be a low amount of money spent on advertising or marketing as your customers will come by recommendations and word of mouth.

Perhaps you would be interested in house cleaning or if you want to work during early morning or evening hours when no one else does, you can focus on office clients.

You could focus on retail businesses and keep your customers clumped into a one or two mile radius. Restaurants are in great need of a daily thorough cleaning and can be a good source of steady clients.

15)   COMPUTER REPAIR

Study the main types of software that system users will require and become completely familiar with all the ISPs (internet service providers) available in the area you intend to cover.
Establish yourself as the expert who can meet the needs of the personal computer user, the small business or a larger corporation.

16)   CONSULTANT

You need to have an expertise in something so you can market yourself as an advisor to others looking to work in that area. Others can learn from the mistakes you have made in the past and more importantly benefit from your best practice. Be careful not to give financial or legal advice unless you are licensed and regulated to do so.

17)   eBay™

I'm proud of how Emyr my youngest son has capitalized on selling items on eBay.

You may have many unwanted items around your household that you could sell on eBay. Research your asking price and decide whether to auction it, buy it now or put it in your eBay store. If auctioning then decide if you want a minimum bid and how long you want the auction to last. You will want to set up a PayPal account to use for transactions.

18)   EDITORIAL SERVICES

Here are some of the editorial services you can provide from the comfort of your own home:

i.   *Copyediting*
This is where fact checking takes place, and where grammatical, stylistic and typographical errors are caught.

ii. **Proofreading**

The proof-reader makes sure the copyediting changes have been properly made and no new errors are created in the process to produce the finished piece.

iii. **Indexing**

There are indexing courses available and you can get indexing software.

iv. **Developmental editing**

A developmental editor works with a manuscript on big picture things like organisation and content issues.

v. **Book doctoring**

This is an editorial service provided for manuscripts written by experts. They create a manuscript as best they can and then a book doctor puts it into publishable shape.

vi. **Ghost Writing**
As a ghost writer, you actually do the research and write the book and someone else's name is attached as the author.

vii. **Copywriting**
Also known as business writing, this is writing that promotes a product or a service.

viii. **Book writing**
Do you have an expertise in a professional area, such as accounting, interior decorating or a craft? Why not write a book about it?

ix. **Magazine article writing.**
Magazines and newspapers are a great way to get your writing published before tackling the daunting task of writing a whole book.

x. *Web page content provider.*
Providing content for a website is a
good way to make some money
writing.

19) ELECTRONICS REPAIR

This is a twofold business similar to the
computer repair business.

You may also want to encourage people to
give you their old electronics so you can use
them for parts

You would need to take on all sorts of
electronic equipment besides just computers.
With smaller electronics, you will need to be
prepared to have customers bring their
repair projects to you, otherwise you would
have the difficulty of recovering the cost of
driving around picking up broken equipment
and returning it.

20) EVENT PLANNING

This is a great 'middle person' business. Do your research and visit every potential event location with which you intend to work.

Visit each site and learn what is available at each location, floor plans, seating quantities, audio visual equipment etc. Populate a database with this information so when you are beginning to plan an event with a client you can find out what the key parameters are for the event and can easily pull up the three or four sites that meet the basic criteria.

21) EXPERT WITNESS SERVICE

One way to make money in this field is by being an expert witness yourself. If you have an expertise that could be useful in legal cases, you can market yourself to attorneys to act as an expert witness. Another way to be active in the expert witness field is to play a sort of matchmaker, matching attorneys up with expert witnesses for their cases, either for the defence or for the prosecution. Expert witnesses for big money cases can be expected to fly anywhere to testify. There's no reason your database of witnesses can't be from all parts of the country.

22) FINANCIAL PLANNER

To begin with, you should go through the certification process so that you can label yourself a CFP (Certified Financial Planner). Your certificate shows that you have expertise and credibility, and this differentiation will help people choose you as their financial planner.

For more information and details on certification, www.cfp.net/become/Steps.asp

23) GOLF COACH

Golfing is a game that business people use to develop relationships outside the office. You do need to be a better than average golfer to develop a reputation as a golf coach. You also need to be a good teacher, know how to be motivational and be willing to work with many different types of people. Let the local public golf courses know about your coaching business. Cultivate relationships with the staff and encourage them to recommend you as a coach.

24) HOME ENERGY AUDITOR

All homeowners are always on the lookout for ways to save on their utility bills. You can come to their aid by providing them with an audit of their house and giving them a breakdown of how they could accomplish real savings in heating, cooling and electrical use. You can go one step further and do the implementation and installation of some of your suggestions in their home yourself. Do a complete appliance audit, with efficiency ratings and calculations based on the age of the appliance. Don't forget the water heater!

25) HOME INSPECTION

You will need to develop contacts with estate agents who can recommend your services to customers. The home inspection field is one where you will need to do constant updating of your skills and knowledge. New products are constantly coming out on the market, if you only know about decks made of wood, you will need to know how to inspect and assess the new materials on the market, such as composites that are made to look like real wood. You will also need to keep informed of all safety updates regarding materials and issues with things like off-gassing, carbon monoxide production, and other chemical precautions.

HOUSEHOLD ORGANISER

You can decide to either do the organising work or to come in to a home and consult on the things the homeowner could do to be better organised. Create checklists and questionnaires to understand how the family uses the home. Are the kids busy with after school activities? Or are they usually home straight after school and want access to their toys? Do they share rooms? All of these things will help you tailor a plan and become the family hero. Have a portfolio of different organisational scenarios in different rooms in the home and talk with the homeowner about the style he or she likes.

26) IMPORT/EXPORT SPECIALIST

If you don't already have work experience with importing and/or exporting, you will have a longer learning curve. You can start by learning the basics and hosting educational sessions to teach others what they need to know to get started in import/export. That alone would probably gain you your first couple of clients. If you keep going with educational seminars and expand your reach to outside your immediate region, you could

probably develop a sufficient and ongoing customer base very quickly.

Ensure that you carry out market research to check demands before purchasing any products to sell. I have witnessed people buying off the Alibaba website only to find they are left with a garage full of products they can't sell!

Be sure to check the import taxes and shipping costs before setting up this business. When systemised correctly this can be a great business. Amazon and eBay can be useful selling platforms for persons at startup who wish to minimize capital outlay.

27) PERSONALISED STATIONERY

If you are artistic then the designs can be themed. Handmade cards and invitations is a great business to start from home.

28)   INTERIOR DESIGNER

A great way to show your portfolio of designs to potential clients is to use an iPad. Design some questionnaires for each chief element and each major room in the house. Find out how the homeowner will use their home. Think about storage, lighting etc. Market your talents to building contractors.

29)   JEWELLERY MAKING

There are many different ways of getting into the jewellery business and many different types of materials with which you can work. Working in metal will probably require the most in the way of specific tools. You need to be able to heat the metal to manipulate it, and you need metalworking tools to cut and engrave it. But there are many other materials that you can work with to make jewellery, such as glass, plastic, beads, feathers, even wood, to name just a few. Making wedding accessory jewellery that can be worn in the bride's hair is a great example of a niche in this business.

30)   MARKETING COPY WRITER

Unless you are already highly experienced working in the copywriting field, take a course. There are online courses or classes at colleges and universities that can give you a leg up in getting experience in writing copy for brochures, catalogues, advertising, and of course marketing copy for the web.

If you can write copy that gets people excited about purchasing what your client has to sell, you can make good money in this business.

31)   WASHING CARS

Location is crucial for maximising customer demand. A well run hand car wash can be an extremely good money spinner and they are relatively easy to set up.

32) COPORATE MASSAGE

Office workers, particularly call centre workers, are very busy and stressed nowadays. Some companies pay for daily massage as part of their occupational health policy to help with productivity at work.

Approach companies and offer this great service which will be appreciated by all. You can also set up a mobile service and don't forget the opportunity to upsell massage oils and related products.

33) VIDEO MARKETING CONSULTANT

Buy professional video making software online. The software these days that makes great sales focused or viral videos is very easy to use and creates very professional videos. These can be uploaded to YouTube and websites and create great value for the clients. Online usage has now surpassed T.V.

It is usually much cheaper than creating a T.V. advert.

34) MARKET FOOD STANDS

People will pay a premium for quality produce. Create an amazing and unique menu and place your name on the waiting list for your local markets for a stand. Perhaps promote a theme like 'Welsh Produce' or 'Fresh from the Farm'.

This can be a great way to get your food brand name out there and also make good money on the product sold.

35) PET SITTER OR WALKER

Many people are too busy with work and need a dog walking or sitting service. You can charge good fees for pet sitting and also walking them daily, if you build a good client base the funds do add up nicely. Also consider a dog grooming service for additional profits.

36) SOCIAL MEDIA CONSULTANT

Take a series of exams by Google which anyone can study, when you pass you will become an AdWords Certified Individual which is awarded by Google, then you will be recommended by them to manage clients' Google AdWords, Google Places. Set up paid advertising for clients and charge a monthly percentage of the spend.

37) LOCAL WALKING TOUR OPERATOR

If you are lucky enough to live in a tourist area and know the locality like the back of your hand you could start up a walking tour. You could show tourists interesting places and areas of outstanding natural beauty or maybe ghost tours.

These are very easy to market on Google
and information centres. This is great for
solid part time work that can turn into a full
time income. Remember to wear a colourful
hat or hold an umbrella so your clients don't
lose you during the walk.

38) MEDICAL EXPERIMENTS

Volunteering for clinical trials doesn't just
have to involve taking untested and risky
drugs. Some clinical trials are perfectly safe,
such as sleep studies, psychological tests and
taste testers. Companies are also always
looking for fit and healthy volunteers living in
London who are willing to donate their blood
for clinical research.
Go to www.Gpgp.net for trials in your
area.

39) PERSONAL CONCIERGE

This business is for someone who is
supremely efficient and has the ability to

make things happen, sometimes the seemingly impossible. People who hire you will expect things when they want them, and you need to be able to come through with not only what they want, but with a personal touch and a smile on your face. The most likely clients for a personal concierge service are top executives who find themselves time starved leaving them very little time to do all those things that often need to be done during the working hours. That's when they turn to (or would like to be able to turn to) professionals to help keep them organised, run errands, and see to it that business and personal obligations are met.

40)   PERSONAL TRAINER

There are only four things you require in order to work as a personal trainer in the UK:

- Level 2 Gym Instructor Qualification
- Level 3 Personal Trainer Qualification

- First Aid Certificate
- Personal Trainer Insurance

Once trained advertise your services in places where everyone goes, like restaurants, supermarkets, gyms etc. Having a website is a good idea, people want some privacy in their decision making when it comes to getting fit. They can go to your website and determine if your approach to personal training is an approach that would work for them. It is important to emphasise the safety aspect of using a personal trainer. You can help clients get fit and avoid injury.

41) BUYING DOMAIN NAMES AND SELLING THEM FOR PROFIT

There are a large number of websites where you can sell domain names for profit. Focus on popular names that companies and businesses would most likely use.

42) REVIEW MUSIC

For the Simon Cowells amongst you check out www.soundout.com, a music website that pays users to review unsigned bands. The idea is simple: you sign up, listen to a track, rate it and write an honest review.

43) PROPERTY MANAGEMENT

Your job, in the case of rental units, will be to make sure the property is running smoothly. For seasonal properties, you will most likely spend your management time making sure the property is ready for seasonal visits and well-maintained when no one is around. If the owners go away for six weeks in the winter, the property manager makes regular checks on the property. You will be the contact number if the security system operator needs to contact someone about a breach in security. This is a business we have set up very successfully and complements our existing property portfolio.

You can charge for tenant sourcing and credit checking for landlords, and engage in a contract with landlords to full letting and management services charged at approximately 10% of rents collected.

44) SMALL ENGINE REPAIR

Most colleges offer some level of engine-repair courses. Another way to learn would be to take a part-time position at a repair shop or a rental facility where you could learn on the job, although you will want to be open about your plans. You should be prepared to work on push lawn mowers, ride-on lawn mowers, generators, garden tools such as rototillers and edgers, chainsaws, wood chippers and snow blowers. You need to decide whether you'll want to take on bigger jobs, such as tractors, snowmobiles and ATVs; space may be your decision maker as you will also need a large storage area to carry out repairs.

45)   SOLAR ENERGY CONSULTANT

As a solar consultant, you basically conduct a home inspection and give clients a report on solar options for their particular home and site. This can range from full-fledged general solar installations that generate electricity to simple solar walkway lighting. You might want to start by working in a solar products company to become knowledgeable in the solar energy field. However, to be a consultant, it is often best not to be affiliated with any one company or product and be able to recommend products and options across the field of solar energy.

46)   VENDING MACHINE BUSINESS

Drinks, snacks, toy grab, cash machine, rides are good for R.O.T.I. I have helped a number of coaching clients set up these businesses very successfully. You can either lease or buy the vending machines depending on your investment funding availability. Nearly

anything can be vended, the important factor
to success is in placing the machines in areas
of highest footfall (number of people walking
past) so that you sell more product. Maybe
pay a pitch fee to shop owners, businesses
and hotels etc to site the machines where
they will be safe, dry and can access electrics.
Vending machines will need a repair man
contact number, then you need to refill them
regularly and collect the cash!

47)   TAXIDERMIST

Get stuffing! Today's world of taxidermy isn't
exclusive to preserving real specimens.
Taxidermy also refers to recreating a
specimen using completely artificial materials.
Taxidermy schools where you can learn the
trade are located throughout the country,
typically as courses over several weeks
specialising in certain levels of expertise, from
beginner to master's level. Like any
enterprise, there are taxidermy events that

you can attend and learn about the latest techniques and materials.

48)   STORAGE BUSINESS

Storing files for businesses or car and boat/house items storage etc.
Consider some significant factors when selecting a location. The size of the land you need will be dependent on how many units you want and the size of them. Additionally, when selecting a location, you should be in a safe area, and close to a large population of potential clientele.

Keep your storage buildings safe. Set up a security system, and offer well lit areas for customers who use the facility at night. A secured entry is expected of all storage facilities.

Document storage where you offer a collect and delivery service for the storing of important documents can prove the most lucrative niche.

One other great business is using shipping containers, spraying them with insulating foam and renting them out for secure storage. We have helped a number of clients make huge profits doing this.

49)   UPHOLSTERING

If you are an expert with a sewing needle, upholstery repair might be a perfect business for you.

One of the best ways to learn how to upholster is to get some discarded upholstered furniture and start tearing it apart. Many books and videos are available to help you learn this trade.

Often furniture ready for upholstering will also need repairs. Have a list available of furniture repair people you can recommend to your customers. Or you can take the piece in, have repair people you work with do this work for you, and add it to the overall cost. You can also learn to do this work yourself, especially minor repairs.

50)   USED BOOK SALES

Almost everyone has a few boxes of books stashed away in the house somewhere. Why not make a business out of them? In order to gain customers, especially repeat customers, you will need to have some regular shop hours. Make your shop known for some specific category (or two) of books, having some first editions for sale, all paperbacks a pound and all hardcovers £2.00 and/or a swap program. Maps, illustrations, postcards, greeting cards and magazines are good side-lines to include in your shop.

51)   TOOTH WHITENING

This requires qualifications but is a service in great demand in the main cities.

52)   WEDDING PLANNER

A mix of an organiser, troubleshooter, designer, diplomat and much more, a wedding planner's precise role is difficult to define. Your job will be to help couples organise the wedding day of their dreams, which means calling up and using a rich mix of skills.

You will need to be up-to-date on wedding trends and fads, dress styles, colour trends, almost everything under the sun! Offer your customers an A la carte menu of services, from helping choose the flowers, the wedding gown and bridesmaid dresses, to picking the venue and hiring the caterer. Before you open your business, visit all the wedding shops, and even pretend you are a bride-to-be, to see what kinds of services the wedding gown shop provides and how they treat potential customers. You need to know every detail of the business to give an accurate impression that you are the go-to person for anyone planning a wedding as well as the ability to think on your feet at all times.

53) HIRE CARS

If you own or have access to a classic car, use it as a wedding car or limousine service. Leasing cars to re-rent out is very profitable if carried out correctly, hence the large number of car and van hire firms present throughout the world.

54) APPLIANCE REPAIR

Every home has a number of appliances, large and small. You can work on your own or on contract with appliance stores to cover their warranty service calls or, best of all, you can do some of each. Plan to start slow and build your customer base on recommendations and referrals based on work well done. Consider developing relationships with contractors to be the expert person to install appliances in newly constructed houses.

55)   MANICURES AND FACIALS

Mobile beauticians can make great profits with little overheads. If you already have your own car then busy professional clients will pay a premium for this handy service. Try to engage clients in contracts for repeat regular business.

56)   LANDSCAPING

Lawns, garden maintenance and general yard clean-up work is always in demand and very easy to set up and market. My son Carwyn made a profit mowing lawns in his first business at seventeen years of age.

57) AFFLIATE PRODUCT SELLING

Find a niche product to sell on the likes of
jvzoo.com or commission junction, rebrand
the product and sell on your niche
information based website you have created.
There are literally millions of products you
can sell on affiliate schemes. Remember the
main 'down' side to this business is you don't
own the equity of the parent company and
you could be making someone else wealthy
other than yourself!

58) EARN FROM WEB RESEARCH

Any Question Answered
(www.issuebits.com), are often on the
lookout for internet researchers. Once a
customer asks a question through their
mobile phone, it's the researcher's job to
hunt out the answer and reply online.

59) COMPUTER TRAINING

If you are an expert in both Macintosh and PC, you could offer training in both types of computers. You could probably make a living helping 'Silver Surfers' learn how to use the internet and e-mail to keep in touch with their loved ones, who are spread around the country.

Err on the side of caution in this business. People do not want to know all the details about what makes a computer work. If you overload them with information from the beginning by explaining bits, bytes, and megapixels, they will stick to their paper and pencil forever.

60) DESKTOP PUBLISHER

You will need strong computer skills, specifically proficiency with desktop publishing software.

A desktop publisher uses computer software to produce publication-ready material including brochures, financial reports, business proposals, menus, books, newspapers, magazines, newsletters, packaging, tickets and business cards. They format and combine text, numerical data, photographs, illustrations and charts.

Alternatively, you can advertise your desktop publishing services to design and create newsletters and books for others with their content.

61)   FENCE INSTALLATIONS

Fences are everywhere. And they don't last forever, so they need to be repaired and replaced with a certain amount of frequency. The most common fence material is wood. However, vinyl has become a popular fence choice due to its longevity and relative freedom from maintenance. Wrought iron is another common fencing, especially in urban environments. You can have fun shopping for vintage wrought iron fencing at salvage yards.

62) LEARN HOW TO ADD HAIR EXTENSIONS

Training costs approximately £400; each customer will pay up to £80. You could forge a deal whereby you place your business in existing hairdressers and pay a percentage of profits for the privilege, that way you would have a good source of customers and little overheads.

63) SURVEYS THAT PAY

The web also offers a wealth of balance-boosting opportunities. Survey websites such as Yougov.com, Panelbase.net and Toluna.com will all reward you for your opinions, either through cash or reward vouchers.

64) FREELANCE GRAPHIC DESIGNER

Despite the proliferation of the internet, print media is here to stay for the foreseeable future! Flyers, newsletters, magazines, information sheets, letters and advertisements are just a few of the types of print media that businesses hire freelancers to create for them.

Websites and online advertising need graphic design services as well.

As a graphic designer, you will need to have a working knowledge of the primary programs in the field. These include Adobe Photoshop, Adobe Illustrator, InDesign, and many others. However, you probably have (or will have) a favourite program that you feel most comfortable with. Use it, and practice with it, as much as you can.

Every good graphic designer is also a student for life. Watch for signs of trends and breakthroughs in the world of graphic design. Look at magazines and newspapers regularly to see what types of designs are popular. Read about current trends online. Never let yourself become out of touch.

Even if your expertise is only in design, offer the works for potential clients, including the editorial creation and the printing and even mailing of the final piece. You can line up regular freelancers for those parts of the job you can't do.

65)   GIFT BASKET SERVICE

A gift basket business can be fun and profitable for a crafty person. Many people start out by signing on with gift basket companies or purchasing business opportunities that require monthly payments. However you don't have to commit to paying monthly fees to get started in this business.

You can build your own gift basket company from scratch. Becoming successful in the gift basket industry may take some planning and time, but you can get started quickly, even if you are on a budget.

Finding a niche is the best way to start out in the gift basket business. Are you a dog lover, horse lover, or exercise guru who could put together baskets that hold the things that people with this interest would like?

If you plan to create baby baskets, you may stock things like infant toys, baby blankets and undershirts, baby lotion, baby powder and soap. For bath baskets, you may need items such as bubble bath, bath salts, bath sponges or cloths, body lotion and candles.

Do you already create a product that a gift basket could be built around? Have you made your own soaps for the past 10 years? A gift basket that included one or two of your soaps, hand lotion, a scrub brush and manicure kit could be a lovely basket to receive.

66) BOTOX/FACIAL AESTHETICS

If you enter the profession of cosmetic surgery, medical spa treatment, or dermatology, then it is essential to obtain your Botox certification. Many centres devoted to beauty offer Botox services, and it is imperative that you receive proper training before administering Botox treatments; however it can be extremely profitable due to the soaring popularity of Botox.

67) GRAFFITI REMOVAL

Create an arsenal of cleaning products that can clean almost every kind of product (paint, chalk, markers) from every kind of surface (cement, wood and pavement). The best way to conduct a graffiti service is to offer a subscription arrangement. Once a month or however often your clients require, go around their property and clean off the graffiti. Charge them a monthly or quarterly fee.

68) HAIRSTYLIST

Hairstyling is a popular business that can be quite lucrative. Generally a home based hairstylist business is likely to be started by someone who has already has a hairstylist career and wants a change. If you already have your hairdressing training and license, and loads of experience under your belt working in a hairstyling salon, you probably have a clientele that will follow you without any hesitation.

69) SELL YOUR OLD CLOTHES

Selling your old clothes for cash is a great way to revamp the wardrobe of your entire family, and to benefit you financially. Are there certain items in your closet which you have worn just once, or maybe never? If you haven't worn it even once in the past year, you will probably never wear it again. Don't clutter your wardrobe by storing these unwanted clothes, they're not likely to be back in fashion again. There are a number of wholesale buyers across the country that pay handsomely for textiles.

70)   HERBAL FARM STAND

Herbs are tremendously popular these days from the smallest shop to the largest discount warehouse, you'll find medicinal herbs, culinary herbs, and herbal teas, baths, candles and aromatherapy essences.

You need to decide whether you will sell your herbs as live plants, picked or cut in bunches and packed, or dried. If you plan to market to cooks instead of gardeners, you will want to sell your herbs either fresh cut and packed in sealed bags, or dried and sold in baggies. You can also consider a "pick-your-own" arrangement; however, be aware that herbs are more delicate than most PYO products. You may save your garden a lot of strife and your plants a lot of wear and tear if you do the picking.

Your customers can be wholesale distributors buying for health product manufacturers, grocery chains and restaurants, or you can sell directly to these businesses yourself

71) DATING AGENCY

A popular business as successful relationships are high on people's needs.

We are rapidly becoming a nation of single people. The well-documented rise in cases of separation and divorce is lining the pockets of lawyers, and is also providing a growing market for online dating sites. According to reports, the majority of people in the UK are single and the online dating industry is turning over thousands.

72) RENT YOUR HOME TO FILM MAKERS

The right kind of property in London can "earn" from £500 a day for a magazine photo shoot to £2,500 a day for a big-budget film.

If you live in an interesting property, you could bag upwards of £1,000 a day renting your home to film and TV companies. To become a regular film backdrop, a property should ideally be inside the M25, have ample off-street parking and offer large rooms with plenty of natural light. Ordinary homes are wanted too.

73) LANDSCAPER

Landscapers create and maintain exterior environments for everything from homes and businesses to parks and government

The
Rich
Rules
Steps to
Wealth &
Happine

buildings. Using knowledge of horticulture, maths, science and landscaping, landscapers make exteriors more attractive and inviting.

Most people want their yards tidied up in the spring, their lawns mown in the summer, their leaves removed in the autumn and their shrubs and driveways ready for winter.

You will also want to offer garden work such as spring planting of annuals and perennials; vegetable garden preparation, planting and autumn clean-up; pest control and watering. You can also offer a tree care service.

74) ESTATE AGENCY/LETTINGS WEBSITE

This is a great business you can run from home. You can run tenant sourcing for landlords and get them to send pictures of their properties to let so you can upload them to main property websites for marketing.

75) TV OR FILM EXTRA

Most major film productions need extras or 'background artists', non-speaking characters to play, for example, the onlookers at a party, customers in a street market or the audience at the Coliseum.

You don't have to look like a supermodel or have the thespian capabilities of John Gielgud. Movies need people of all ages and shapes and sizes. Acting experience, even in school plays or amateur dramatics, helps but is not essential.

You could make up to £150 a day. You will need to join an agency first.

76) MOVING SERVICE

Starting a removals company is very easy. For smaller jobs such as bedsits and flats you'll just need a medium-sized van and any materials to secure fragile items inside, alongside essentials such as insurance. The main additional cost will be marketing and promotion as it'll be difficult to drum up business by word-of-mouth only. Whilst the majority of removals contracts will inevitably come from local residents, business owners are able to look further afield, increasing the potential for revenue.

77) BURGER, ICE CREAM VANS, TRAILERS

Large potential profits if sited in high footfall areas. We run ice cream vans and trailers; the most profit we make is £4000 per month! Very good returns when located in the main shows and events, work out the cost of the pitch and potential sales before signing contacts with show organisers.

78) MUSIC LESSONS

You want to stick to the instrument(s) you know, but you may be a skilled enough musician to offer lessons on several different instruments, or those in a particular class, e.g. stringed or woodwind. You can decide to take on individuals or classes, depending on space and availability of instruments.

What is it that makes your teaching business special? Perhaps you will make recordings for students to take home. Maybe you will coach an ensemble and direct recitals for friends and family to attend.

79) AUCTION WEBSITES

As stated previously, there are a large number of sites that pay affiliate commissions or you can buy and sell products through websites. I use this approach to trade cars and motorbikes.

80) PHOTOGRAPHER

In order to get hired by someone who isn't a close family member or friend, you will need to have a portfolio built up to show off your best work. Use photographs from multiple shoots with different subject matter to show the range of your talents. Make sure that your portfolio is comprised of more than just five or ten photos; people will want to see the great work you've done.

Making money as a photographer can be done in a number of different ways. You can specialise in one area, the most common being weddings. There are niches you can explore for photography - portraits of people and their pets, families, and homes; photographs of holiday events, birthday parties or for Christmas cards; the possibilities are endless.

81) TICKET RESELLING WEBSITES

Now you can make money buying and selling tickets at home, using online brokers.

It is best to make all your sales using online brokers that make sure sales are in compliance with any local laws.

Perhaps the biggest and best-known of the online platforms is StubHub.com, which also guarantees the tickets for the buyer, alleviating their concerns about fakes. This makes it easier for you to sell.

82)   RENT OUT A PARKING SPACE

Depending on your area, you could net up to £200 per month (more in some places, e.g. parts of London) just for letting somebody park in your drive or garage. The most covetable spaces tend to be in city centres, but you can still make serious cash elsewhere.

If you live by a big transport link such as an airport or railway station, or even a football ground, you're sitting on a potential goldmine.

The
Rich
Rules
Steps to
Wealth &
Happiness

83) RUG CLEANING

You will need to learn how to work with all
kinds of carpet fabrics, from synthetic to
wool carpets. Decide whether you will take
on valuable antique carpets and family
heirlooms; if so, you will want to get
specialised training in how to handle these
carpets and the specialised ways of cleaning
them. Learn how to get tough stains and
odours out of carpets such as dog and cat
smells and your services will be in great
demand.

84) CREATING WEBSITES

Outsourcing this work to countries where
it's more cost effective can be lucrative for all
parties. The service of website building is
generally cheaper in Asia, Philippines, India
and China. You can be the 'middle' person
and sell into countries where websites cost
more.

85)   BED AND BREAKFAST

Do you have a room that has its own bathroom and is private from the rest of the living space? Are you near attractions such as a tourist area, sports stadium or venue for a large annual event? Or is your home in the country, offering a city-dweller a weekend of peaceful living? Say you can rent the room for £150 a night for Friday and Saturday nights 48 weeks a year, that's £14,400 in revenue! Utilise what you have and create a unique experience.

86)   CHRISTMAS TREE SALES

If you're looking for a profitable cash crop for a small acreage, consider growing Christmas trees. They are a low maintenance crop, ideal for a spare time project, and can produce a good income for years to come. By planting a portion of your acreage with new trees each year, it will provide a steady income as the trees mature in an average of eight years and are harvested and replanted.

You may be surprised to learn that the market for live Christmas trees is growing, as the buying public is turning its back on plastic artificial trees in favour of the 'real thing.' Sales of artificial trees peaked in 2007, and have been declining since.

Selling your trees yourself is the best option. Consumers come to the property, pick the one they want, and you fell it for them.

87) RECYCLE OLD MOBILE PHONES

There are a number of online websites where we can sell our old phones. Old iPhones for example can command a price of up to £150

88) RENT A ROOM

You may know of a spare room and can create an agency to rent it out. Alternatively convert a section of your home to segregate an area to create a private letting room.

89) CLAIM ALL TAX CREDITS

We can create a business whereby we help clients by raising their awareness of any tax incentives and reliefs available to them. However at no time will we provide legal or financial advice; we will also introduce them to a specialist tax advisor who can help them with direct advice when necessary. There are huge amounts of unclaimed tax credits, a good tax advisor is essential in advising us of all our entitlements. A great website in the UK is entitledto.co.uk

90) CREATE AN ACCELERATED DEBT REPAYMENT PLAN

One of the requests we often have is to help both our tenants and business customers with their finances and budgeting and clearance of debt. A business can be created whereby we can help people by showing them the options to creating an accelerated debt repayment plan. However for compliance and customer safety, so that we are not giving direct advice to our customers, we associate with an independent financial advisor who will speak directly to the customer. Any resultant fees charged to the customer for this service could also include fees charged by the independent financial advisor. It's a shame that we were not taught efficiently in school, further, and higher education, in how to simply run a home or to budget properly in our personal and business lives. This leads to a shortfall in people's knowledge.

One self-employed client got herself out of debt and paid off her mortgage within three years, using this strategy combining off set mortgages, accelerated debt repayment and 0% money transfers. Being self-employed the client was saving for tax and paying the money into a savings account off set against her mortgage. She began paying down her debts starting with the highest interest rate first, once one paid off she added these payments to paying off the next highest interest rate, and carried on until she had paid off all her debts. Once all the debts were cleared she paid the same amount that she had been using to pay off her debts into her off set mortgage. In addition to this she strategically used 0% credit cards, also paid into her off set mortgage, to pay off her mortgage within three years.

91) CAR BOOT SALES

Either run one or attend one and sell items. My children make approximately £200 profit at each one!

92) GET PAID FOR YOUR HOBBY

If you have a hobby such as painting, DIY, restoring machines, other people will pay you to do what you would do for love.

93) CLASSIC CAR & MOTOR PARTS TRADING

Buy scrap cars, dismantle, sell parts then weigh in the shell and broken parts for scrap. Often times the monies we receive for the scrap can cover the initial purchase price of the scrap car.

94) MUSIC FESTIVAL CHILL OUT TENT WITH RESCUE PACK

Create your own rescue pack to sell e.g. to include an energy drink, Berocca, Cagoule, pack of tissues and wipes.

95) CARBON FIBRE COATINGS OF MOTOR PARTS

A specialist but simple effective business. You can buy a Carbon Fibre Skinning Starter Kit which contains everything you need to take an original part (made from plastic, metal or any other material) and cover it with genuine 2/2 twill carbon fibre and finish it to a high gloss.

96) MYSTERY SHOPPER

With cashback sites you can earn even more money from shopping online. Google cashback websites, they will automatically pay you every time you buy a product or a service from selected retailers, from your weekly groceries to switching your utility provider.

97) CHILD-FRIENDLY APPS

Children are your future customers so gaining their loyalty now is a great idea.

The connectivity of children is a big trend for 2015. Three quarters of children have access to a mobile device. This suggests a huge business opportunity for anyone who can create products or design apps just for children. It would also be a good idea if the app is educational or promotes good health as this will also appeal to the parents.
Start small by designing a few child-friendly apps and see where your business takes you.

98) EMPLOYEE MONITORING SERVICES

Employees are increasingly mobile due to flexi time contracts, sales representatives etc. In fact, it is estimated there will be 1.3 billion mobile workers by 2015.

How do employers keep track of their employees' time and what they are doing? There are many business opportunities for vehicle tracking time clocks and time clock apps. Also employers don't have the time, money or staff to manage all this new information and process it for payroll and billing.

A business that could provide employee monitoring services, as well as some additional outsourced human resources and payroll functions, would be in great demand.

99)   INK AND TONER CARTRIDGE REFILLING

Businesses that can provide ink and toner cartridge refilling can save companies a lot of money and also help protect the environment from unnecessary waste.

Some of the benefits of starting an ink and toner cartridge refilling business include:
It's good for the environment because it reduces cartridges in landfills.
The start-up costs are relatively low and there are start-up kits available to help you get started, also franchise opportunities available.
Your business can be home-based, mobile or have satellite locations. You have a broad target market and can service individual residences or businesses; also there is a growing demand for refillables.

$\mathcal{R}$ich $\mathcal{R}$ule 10

Take Control

Taking control has been the most significant factor that has contributed to my success. Learning that I must take responsibility for my own actions and not lay blame on others for my outcomes is key to **Rich Rule 10**

In my scholarship study I realised that the main difference between most people and entrepreneurs is that entrepreneurs don't just talk about what they want to do, they take control of their lives and actually implement their thoughts and feelings into action.

Myself and all leading entrepreneurs that I know, are often termed control freaks as we have to become leaders in not only controlling our own lives but also our outcomes.

Taking control of your own direction does not mean you have to become a dictator, it means that you have clarity of vision of exactly what your outcomes (goals) are and a clear action plan to achieving them, whatever it takes.

There have been times in my life where I have had no sleep whatsoever for two consecutive days and nights as I am so committed to achieving certain outcomes. This is a typical trait in every successful entrepreneur I know.

Taking control, however, is not a natural trait in most successful entrepreneurs as we tend to be slightly introverted and don't wish to be leading from the front. Empowerment is therefore extremely important to us whereby we share our outcomes with others on our team to achieve results.

This sounds easy in theory but is often not as easy in practice, therefore we do have to "control the environments in which we work using proven systems in order to guarantee success".

In my life journey I have always wanted to be the best that I can be which includes up-skilling myself in all areas of life and business. Like many entrepreneurs I have invested a huge amount of time, effort and money in improving myself. I won't engage in any business activity or life time activity without fully researching and learning about it first. On occasions during the research process this proposal may not feel right so I will not continue following that path.

By listening to my intuition when it does feel right, the knowledge and awareness gained through research and education provide me with more confidence to strive forward, take control, and start that life activity or business.

I could not have achieved all that I have to date without up-skilling myself, again this is common with all entrepreneurs, and we never stop learning and striving for knowledge in all areas of our lives that we love.

As a personal thank you from me I have a gift for you to help you achieve success in your life to becoming **Wealthier and Happier.** I want to give you a winning start with complimentary access to the key information that has helped me to succeed.

There are two ways in which you can gain access to this information.

1. Please send me a personal email to kevin@therichrules.com referencing the Rich Rules Complimentary Steps. Please supply your preferred contact telephone number, full name and address.

Or

2. You can tear off and complete one of the two FREEPOST cards which are inserted at the back of this book. Please pass the other FREEPOST card to a trusted friend or colleague whom you wish to help.

My team will then respond accordingly and signpost you to the gateway for all educational information.

You will receive complimentary access to learning steps that will help you apply Rich Rules principles in your own life to help you start up or improve your business or multiple businesses using my own well proven methods. I will also send you software templates for working the numbers as a special thank you for following **The Rich Rules.**

During my journey to **Wealth and Happiness** I have received a large amount of help from leading entrepreneurs, I am extremely grateful to all of them who have contributed to helping me. Now it's my time to repay their kindness by helping you.

*G*ratitude

A special thanks to my parents for putting up with me over the years and they have always been there for me and the children.
Sandie, my close friend and healer who has kept my feet on the ground.
All my team and office staff who have helped to run and grow our businesses whilst maintaining happy dispositions.
My fourteen pet donkeys that have listened to my views but never judged!

NB. All calls are recorded for training and monitoring purposes.

I really appreciate feedback highlighting your success as a result of following the Rich Rules steps, please let me know personally by emailing

kevin@therichrules.com

Wishing you all that you wish for yourselves.

Kind regards

MR K.A. Green

Kevin Green

To contact Kevin please see
www.kevingreen.co.uk

For PR/Media enquires please email
wealth@mooving.org

Or

Telephone 0044 (0)1554 833330.

FREEPOST
KEVIN GREEN WEALTH